P£aying on a Shoe$tring

P£aying on a Shoe$tring

'sporting bachelor at large'

Nigel Kenyon

NUNC AUT NUNQUAM

FENWICK PUBLICATIONS

PUBLISHED BY
FENWICK PUBLICATIONS

P.O. Box 2121, Shrewsbury SP2 4WB

First Published 2006
Copyright © Nigel Kenyon 2006

ISBN 0-9554190-0-X   978-0-9554190-0-3

Printed in Great Britain by
Biddles Ltd, King's Lynn, Norfolk

Contents

CONTENTS

Preface

'Each playboy in the world whips the same top on a different axis' (Sale)

On the back of 'you should write a book', 'what an interesting life you've had' and other such platitudes, I have put together another book, this time about me.

Autobiographies can be a string of chronological events getting duller by the minute, or a fabrication of half-truths incorporating other people's jokes or experiences. There is a further kind of 'wannabe' or 'wish I had' written as fiction. I can at least assure the reader that the following story is the truth, albeit in the context of a family who has established 'gut' over several centuries. This priming in the pump has provided me with a platform to exist, and then channel various gifts and energy down selected paths, for better or worse, richer or poorer.

Aware of the above, my story is blended with some relevant social and family history.

I have sidelined this mix into my own opinions and commentary – getting bees out of the bonnet – as to how I find the changing scenes of life have not only affected me, but also Mr & Mrs G.B. Everybody.

'You must remember, Nigel, that you and I are dinosaurs' – as told to me some years ago.

I make no apologies for any recognisable plagiarised expressions or bons mots – they always get found out – but there are a few NK originals… maybe. Also, in order to save any undue embarrassment, particularly amongst the ladies, I have only used proper names in general context, and when on neutral ground. If you think it's you, please smile at least, 'if only' is purely personal! That's the sex aspect. Religion and politics will take care of themselves, whilst let's draw on the money side of things, remembering the Presbyterian adaptation of the Lord's Prayer, 'Forgive us our debts as we forgive our debtors.'

As far as acknowledgements go, you will note no corny references to advice from old pals, friendship, inspiration, relentless overtime by long-suffering secretaries, or support from a wife 'sharing my world'. No, with the exception of consultation with the shaving mirror, which often does invaluable service for a committee, the following chapters, sometime assembled as stories within the Story, are by me.

However, a big thanks to my producer and designer John Saunders, Jackie Pritchard copy editor, and printers Biddles Ltd. of King's Lynn. The rest, including sales strategy and structure, has been match-managed by… well done, you guessed!

NB. The opinions of the author do not necessarily reflect those of any persons depicted in the text or illustrated in the photographs. This also includes any patrons, directors or their employees, of businesses featured in the appendices.

Introduction

'Even he, the minute makes immortal, proves, perchance,
but mortal in the minute' (Browning)

Whilst the NK life story is reported entirely on personal experience and information direct from living third parties and close relations, I feel that an exposé of a previous generation of great-grandparents on both sides of my parents' families will reinforce the basis of the 'gut'. Similar to horses and dogs this is something we all have, alongside the two great free gifts of flair and imagination, and it evolves accordingly.

From early childhood one always heard of 'the Mill'. This was several mills, at one point totalling six, which were based in and around Bury in the county of Lancashire. Having started as an established business in 1664 as fullers and woollen cloth merchants from a background of yeoman farmers, the Kenyons (James Kenyon & Son Ltd.) were engaged in the textile industry for ten unbroken generations, celebrating a tercentenary in 1964. [b1]

However, the chain was nearly broken in 1863 when the then James Kenyon died unexpectedly with his son just having reached his seventeenth birthday. With a marketplace in industrial cloths and papermakers' felts expanding fast in the general mid-Victorian explosion of

British industrial thrust, his widow Margaret was left with a difficult choice. Her decision, backed by all hands and senior mill manager 'Old Tweedle': to take control and run things until my great-grandfather James Kenyon was accepted as the active head of the firm. He took over having not quite reached his twentieth birthday!

By all accounts JK was an austere and unbending man, but always scrupulously fair in his dealings. From his earliest days he had been active in sport and games. For a cricket match in Bury he brought in the first Australian team that included Aborigines, he owned race-horses, was a good shot and hunted with the Holcombe Hunt.

He expanded the business rapidly for the rest of the nineteenth century, right on till his death in 1924. He was able to communicate with his employees and in 1897 'the Guv'nor' was elected as Conservative-Unionist MP for Bury. He was a fine public speaker, often handling hecklers with pithy riposte, in a broad Lancashire accent, bringing roars of laughter from the audience. His representation of Lancashire's powerful presence at that time in the British economic structure was significant in the passing of such bills as the Education of Children and the Factory and Workshops Act of 1902, when he resigned. Alongside all this machismo, JK had married in 1876.

His wife, Elise, was German. Her family were prosperous industrialists in Karlsruhe, and she met JK through her brother who represented Kenyon's for trade in Russia. She immediately adopted the role of brood mare, common in Victorian times, by bearing ten children of which five survived! – Jimmy, Charles (my grandfather), Geoffrey, Myles, and Josephine. All feature in later chapters bar Jimmy, who died in 1919 as a result of gas in the First World War trenches.

Apart from being musical as a very gifted pianist, Elise was popular with everybody, and the affection which she lavished on her own family was extended to the working folk of the Kenyon mills. She was drawn into many of their social activities, and could be seen supporting both football and cricket, often as the scorer, on the grounds which had been set aside for the purpose around their family home.

Walshaw Hall, now an old folk's home, is a typical neo-Gothic pile befitting the style of an old-established industrial family. Standing on a ridge, 3 miles from Bury, and surrounded by a large garden and the fields, the house of some twenty bedrooms boasted a vast dining room, billiard room and other day rooms to match. A key feature for the children was a gigantic nursery which was equipped with toys, a piano and even a full-scale swing and rope ladder. This was a house of happiness for all, and hardly anyone from outside was turned away without a hearing. If Elise was at home this could mean help with money or food.

My grandmother's father, Thomas Statter, albeit a Lancastrian, was out of a different 'mould' as compared to James Kenyon. For rather hazy reasons his family had always been connected with the earls of Derby, and he himself was agent to the 16th and 17th earls. As the Derbys owned great tracts of Lancashire, including major portions of towns such as Bolton and Bury, business trips often meant a week away (travelling by coach, don't forget) and setting up 'shop' in a hotel for meetings. Statter's knowledge of the countryside and rural affairs was always at cutting edge, and consequently the visiting team were known as 'Lord Statter and Mr Derby'. He was also interested in all countryside activities, particularly shooting, and was one of the founding group who established the English Setter and Pointer dog breeds as we know them today. [b2]

In 1887 his brother and family had emigrated to the United States and established land ownership in the Midwest, controlled from their home in Sioux City, Iowa. Thus the American Connection was established and will feature strongly later on in my story.

My mother's family was entirely Scottish, which emanated on both sides from a variety of sound middle-class, professional stock. Her mother, Agnes, had married in her early twenties, only to be widowed in the First World War when her husband Captain Stoute's ship was sunk while on active service. This was the moment for her father, Donald Matheson, to adopt a paternal role for his two granddaughters.

Matheson was a man of visionary and pioneering spirit, which backed the hard-headed businessman approach to capture the front row of the ever expanding leisure market. As General Manager of the Caledonian Railway Company (later to be amalgamated with the London, Midland & Scottish) he had a belief that if you had travellers in your pocket on the train, you might as well keep them in your pocket when they finished the journey. This led to the development of city-based Railway Hotels, which then expanded the theme into the countryside, particularly in Scotland. The flagship, Gleneagles, was opened in 1924 to unanimous acclaim from the Press: 'The Playground of the Gods', 'The Switzerland of Scotland', and 'The Highland Palace'. The following (with some editing and family addition from yours truly – the contributor) appears in a 75 years commemorative book published in 1999. [b3]

"Mr Matheson was a truly extraordinary man, living a lifestyle that has long since faded into distant memory. Nigel Kenyon recalls the manner in which Donald Matheson and his wife Agnes travelled when King George V and Queen Mary were due at Balmoral. Grandfather and granny had a town residence as a permanent suite in the Central Hotel in Glasgow. When they wished to travel, the stationmaster would escort them to their own train which consisted of a day and a night carriage, a guards van and two engines to help push the larger convoy over Shap on return from London.

Once in London, the Royal Train of five carriages was hitched into the middle and off to the Highlands. Somewhere around Watford an equerry would appear with a message 'Their Majesties request the pleasure of the company of Mr & Mrs Matheson for dinner.' This involved dining with two rather unsociable people around a table the size of a small card table. [r1]

It was an enduring friendship, however, and when Matheson MVO (Member of the Victorian Order) died in 1935, the following telegram was sent to his widow. 'The King and Queen much regret to hear of the death of Mr Donald Matheson, of whom they preserve many pleasant recollections. Their Majesties assure you and your family of their true sympathy in your bereavement.'

The bond between Matheson and the King and Queen came from a meeting of minds. Donald Matheson was a very charming and kind man, but he found it difficult to relate to people on an emotional level. When his son-in-law was lost in the First World War, he took on paternal responsibility for his two granddaughters, Agnes and Ailsa, and sent them to be educated at Cheltenham Ladies College. His letters to them [which I have seen] were full of details of business and board meetings, rather than tales of the family pets and other stories likely to amuse and interest young girls. One thing which did surface, however, was the close friendship between Matheson and Sir Robert McAlpine [founder of the McAlpine construction dynasties]. In one letter he wrote, 'Stuart [Matheson's son] and Alfred and Robert [Sir Robert's sons] are getting on so well that we are thinking of forming a joint company.' Stuart's untimely death in 1926 prevented this from happening, and had the effect of Matheson withdrawing into himself and becoming rather reclusive.

Granny Matheson [as I knew her when she visited us in Cheshire after the Second World War, before dying in 1947. Who could forget the formidable, Persian lamb-clad figure sashaying down the Crewe platform, surrounded by the Stationmaster and a team of porters?] enjoyed the luxurious lifestyle, but was rather naïve when it came to the ways of the world. When Gleneagles first opened she would often sit outside the front door greeting guests and friends alike as though it were her own personal home!"

Donald Matheson's second daughter, Florence (Aunty Fluff), never married, and it was his granddaughter Agnes who married my father Derek Kenyon in 1939. The wedding took place at Granny Matheson's country home, Hall House in Fenwick, and my father's diary would have read as follows.

Played a round of golf at Troon early a.m., hole-in-one at 126 yards Postage Stamp, wedding service and reception Fenwick p.m. Evening progress to Gleneagles in my Mk V Bentley, to be greeted by Glasgow evening paper on hall-porter's desk with a large picture of Agnes and self leaving the church. Following morning further wedding disclosure when I whipped my driver out with a flourish on the first tee, surrounded by friends and caddies, and we were all covered in confetti!

I have included this last piece of 'history', as readers will see how it blends into the first chapter and beyond.

[b1] See appendix 'Interesting Books & Other References' [r1].

1 In the Beginning...

'All the world's a stage'   (Shakespeare)

... God created the heaven and the earth, and at 9.30 p.m. on the 20th January 1941 Charles Nigel Kenyon, at Hall House, Fenwick, Ayrshire. The day had been dramatic!

With Dad away supporting the War in the Coldstream Guards, my mother Agnes had retreated to her grandmother's home in Scotland. She was accompanied by her sister Ailsa who was also a war widow, her husband serving as a regular naval officer. On the morning of the historic day they went for a drive on Fenwick Moor (four months later the landing site of Hitler's deputy Rudolf Hess), when mist and thick snow blew in, quickly creating very hazardous conditions which were virtually impassable for a little Morris 8 with a scrounged half gallon of petrol in the tank.

My mother, who was of a more nervous disposition than her stoical sister, started to panic and suddenly 'I think something's starting to happen', only to be met with a spontaneous reply, 'Well, you'd better hang on till we get off this bloody moor.' This was easier said than done in howling blizzard conditions, made more difficult with Hall House standing down a valley, by the side of the village, at the end of a long private drive. Guthrie the gardener dug like mad, the district nurse/midwife just made it, whilst the doctor had to abandon his car in the village and haul himself through the waist-deep snow. However, the accompaniment of many postnatal drams and supper signified that we had all delivered! I was immediately supported by the nanny culture. A seriously starched nurse, Miss Greeve, took charge.

Why not? I am very certain that the whole question is a matter of selection. Top of the tree are the formally trained Norland, Princess Christian, or Chiltern variety. Next the college girl trained in child-care, then mother's helps and au pairs a poor third. They are not servants and, for best results, need controlling at all levels by someone who has had experience on the receiving end and been brought up in similar surroundings. Au pairs are usually a dead loss and wind up as a bit on the side for dad. Such comments from younger mums as 'I am against nannies' usually mean that they cannot afford one, bearing in mind that child day care can currently cost up to £20,000 p.a., making boarding school look relatively very good value. The classic summary of someone in control must be from a very grand young mum (aka Lady Wah Wah) when being grilled by her girlfriends around the lunch table as to her course of action re her husband's indiscretion: 'Why, sack nanny of course, one can't have that sort of behaviour at the Hall.'

In 1942 we moved back to Cheshire to my parents' home, Blackden Manor. Blackden is an Elizabethan house dated 1592, with early nine-teenth-century additions which in no way spoil the earlier front. The barns in the separate farmyard are dated 1709, and extend into the Cheshire countryside surrounds. This pocket battleship is still main-tained today by my brother Donald and his wife Isobel as a true family house.

The nursery was taken over by Nanny Oscher. Dressed in dark blue, a white starched apron literally crackling, her dark hair rolled back into a tight bun and looking at us from behind spectacles, our Swiss German nanny looked formidable to say the least, never mind strict. She was firm, but of such a disposition that we naturally got on with her.

'Pussycat was machst du?' was as far as she needed to go for 'I don't like that one bit and don't you do it again.' I say 'we' in this context as my mother's sister had produced my first cousin, Fiona, and they had come to live with us.

Nanny had a German-speaking ally in Margaret Weiss the cook. Margaret had been shipped out of Austria in 1938 by her parents, and she never saw them again! She was a fantastic cook, able to make wonderful cakes, puddings, and pies out of practically nothing and a few rationing coupons. These ingredients were supported by vegetables from the garden and poultry, whose output extended to anyone connected with the house. My mother, who could speak passable German, had also been a great comfort to Margaret, climaxing in early 1946 when 'telephone for Margaret': her boyfriend of years back had made it, was in London, and freed from refugee status. Excitement all round, and she was immediately packed off on the train to meet up with him… subsequently to start an eaterie in North London, obviously as husband and wife!

Nanny Oscher moved on to help my aunt, who by this time had bred three more daughters and established her own house with her husband who had retired from the navy. There was a rare gloom around for a few days when we learned that our Swiss nanny had been killed in an avalanche whilst skiing during a vacation with her parents. They lived in the mountains on a smallholding farm, a far cry from the more sophisticated environment she had been involved with whilst with us.

My brother Donald had turned up in June 1944 in the same room where he sleeps today, and a new nanny later appeared in the shape of Nanny Etheridge, and for shape one could say curvaceous. This was very apparent when she accompanied us on holiday to Scotland and changed from/into her birthday/bathing suit on the beach at Troon, with Mum and Dad playing golf on Royal Troon just behind the dunes. This handsome Jane Russell lookalike even caught the eye of a 6-year-old, and I never know what prompted me to whack such a magnificent sunbathing behind as hard as I could with my toy spade! She resigned soon after and, as I was shortly on my way to boarding school and my brother had been learning fast as the backmarker, the nursery policy was redirected to the mother's help angle. A succession followed, all Swiss, who acted as a companion for him and kept an eye on me during the holidays.

Further indoor support for the house was sergeant-majored by Mrs Whitehurst. She arrived on a vintage black, steel-framed lady's bicycle, on the dot and in any weather. As a very much hands-on, down and scrub type, she gave a reluctant lead to Hutchie. The latter, Miss Hutchinson, had been a personal lady's maid in Scotland for mother's family and was also an expert seamstress. General housework was a bit of a comedown, but her sewing capabilities were harnessed not only for us all, but also locals and war efforts for the WVS (Women's Voluntary Services). Mrs Whitehurst was engrossed with poultry and could pluck and dress a goose in a few minutes, never mind a chicken or a pheasant. Her shed at the back of her little cottage was always filled with feathers, whilst her garden was a haven for fruit. Gooseberries were a big feature for the local show, highlighted one year with an example which was claimed as a world record – the size of a cricket ball!

Outside, the gardens were the pride of Clifford Broome. Broome worked at Blackden all his life, having started as garden boy aged 14. The 'three Rs' were virtually non-existent, but his knowledge seemed limitless, and very much his own. Roses were pruned from February 1st regardless, and he took special interest in the areas of the bulb garden, the water garden, and herbaceous borders. The yew tree walls and features divided the show gardens from the vegetables. These were extensive and beautifully laid out, extending to fruit trees espaliered onto the house. The nursery overlooked this side of things and one could literally pluck plums from the windows. I once decided to see if I could climb down the outside of the house on these bushes, fortunately to be apprehended at the start.

Mowing machines and general maintenance did not come into Broome's vocabulary, and woe betide anyone picking anything. All vegetables were sourced by him only and flowers were only to be cut by him or my mother… her knowledge passed the test. A real scene blew up when his prize marrows were vandalised by the evacuees.

The latter, four lads from Liverpool, were billeted in a wing and overseen by Jane, a retired housekeeper who left when they did. The close proximity to a simple, but friendly, village school and the wonderful country environment must have provided a real bonus out of adversity. Later we were visited at various stages of their lives to show off wives and children, and I remember 'Billy' turning up in a huge lorry. He had started his own transport business and this was merely one of a substantial fleet.

Young scousers also featured at a local Approved School (aka Reform School or Borstal) of which Dad was a governor. He rightly took this role seriously, to the extent of going round on Christmas Day to help carve and supervise the inmates' Christmas dinner. We had to accompany him on school sports days to show the family spirit, and also to give one an idea of what happened to young miscreants who had been pulled out of Liverpool, Manchester and other local cities. War had obviously led to family break-ups and heightened criminal tendency in very obvious areas such as Bootle and Moss Side.

Dad, having been a quarter-mile pacemaker for Harold Abrahams, enjoyed helping Colonel Brown, the firm but fair headmaster, setting up the day. Parents attended, but not all was jolly good fun.

I have never forgotten eavesdropping on the following exchange between a fifteen-stone mum, a half-pint dad and their son. He was lean as a whippet, and had just run in a race, all dressed in his regulation issue singlet, shorts and black plimsolls. 'Well, Tommy, we've 'eard from the 'edmasster, and me an yer Dad 'ere, can oonly say that if yer don't do better, we won't be 'avin yer back.' Whaaat! I was dumbfounded. No more home, what was he going to do? Tommy said nothing, his face tightened up and his bright blue eyes sparkled. This was pure, justified hatred, as sad as that. Talk about reflecting on home.

'Outside' extended to the fields and general countryside, where haymaking and harvesting were the great feature… all sheaves, stooks and real horsepower. Tractor power started in 1952 with a small Ferguson. I enjoyed driving this, and was a useful ally to our farmer Mr Curbishley, son Harold and their hand Tom. I only once had the trailer stacker flying off the back due to an unscheduled start!

The next phase of staff at the house, after retirement of Broome, Margaret and several short-termers, ushered in Elsie in the kitchen and John as head gardener. Elsie (Miss Worthy) came from Bury and had been a cook for my great-aunt Maggie for many years. On the latter's death, Elsie's life was decided for her around the breakfast table when Maggie's estate was being discussed by my father. 'We do not want the summer house in Anglesey [big mistake], we'll retire Harold [her chauffeur] on a small pension and give him the car, and what shall we do with Elsie?' 'No problem,' says mother, 'she can come here as the cook.'

The mill van was briefed and Elsie arrived with her few possessions and little suitcases.

She stayed at Blackden for some fifteen years, till she retired to a trailer home in the village. These were council controlled and virtually free issue, but only for bona fide lifetime residents of the village. Dad paid her entry fee and our Doctor was able to fix the qualification aspect.

John and his wife Emily, who came in to help in the house and help my mother in her role as County Organiser for the WRVS as a platoon sergeant, were installed in a newly converted cottage in the barns, and with us till retirement. He was very well read and crazy on growing chrysanthemums as his own specialist hobby. Each Sunday evening this Lancastrian trio could be seen, dressed in Sunday best, wending their way to evening service to follow their deep-rooted Methodist form of Christianity.

I have left two more outside characters for a later chapter. They were also from the same mould as these other fine people who I was lucky enough be helped by at the start.

2 Educating Nigel – Phase 1

'Manners maketh man' (Winchester College)

… and I often think 'woman as well, they cost nothing and never did anyone any harm'. But they were basics that were on the must do list from the word go. From the parents, the nursery, wherever, good manners were constantly being fed into the gut.

As I was an only one at the time, simple nursery play-schooling was advanced to serious governess teaching at 3 years old. This took place in a private house and was shared amongst five families. The class was composed of six girls and me, all older, except for our hosts' younger daughter, Jane, who quickly became my ally. Our pretty governess, Miss Darlington, lived at her parents' smallholding farm on the then edge of Goostrey village. She later married a local who became a successful dealer in the new world of TV and white goods.

Lessons were a serious affair which began at nine sharp, half an hour's break at eleven, and heads down again till twelve-thirty. This started as a three-day-a-week event for us smalls, graduating to five mornings and full days thereafter, based on a standard three term schedule. Subjects, skilfully graded for the age gaps, extended from the 'three Rs' to geography, history and scripture, model making and some drama made up for hobbies. A notable production of 'Father Christmas [me] comes to supper' must have awakened the family performing instinct.

Playtime was always fun either inside or out. In our first venue there was a steep staircase running up from the centre hallway, and it was here that I had my first sexual experience, brought about as a voyeur. Girls first and bouncing up the stairs made for an upskirts visual of pretty knickers, and consequential 'stirring in the loins' as I discovered, all quickly brushed aside at the first time of enquiry. 'It sometimes happens with little boys' – and big ones too, I'd have thought!

Our hosts moved house and school followed. Their large garden, surrounded by a terrace fortified with old guns poking out of a battle-mented wall, and a desecrated chapel, made an excellent backdrop for fun. (I was next involved with the chapel some thirty-five years later when I helped the owner, a personal friend, by bringing in a choir to back up a re-consecration service. The whole building had been completely restored, ready for bishops, unaccompanied choral even-song, followed by champagne supper… a far cry from the roofless shell playground.) Sadly our hosts and two of my classmates, their daughters Anne and Jane, were killed in a plane crash, and school moved to our home at Blackden.

Fortunately, through my father's natural ability and enthusiasm, games and other extra-curricular school activities were not over-looked. Ladies' hickory-shafted golf clubs were shortened to enable a proper shot and lightweight tennis racquets had grips modified. The latter provided for plenty of fun in the courtyard at the centre of the house, where we could be gated in and yet visible from any wing of the quadrangle. A dear spaniel, who chased the ball to the extent of frenzy, made up the party. A grass tennis court gave one a start at the real thing.

Apart from the constant emphasis on behaving, another 'social

With Nanny and Dad

Fiona: "On your bum again cousin Nigel"

With Mum

(*top left*)
James Kenyon,
M.P., J.P.

(*above*)
Charles Kenyon with
'Rusty'

(*left*)
Derek Kenyon

Nigel Kenyon
(*Photo: Glyn Satterley*)

Philip Kenyon

COTHILL HOUSE

(*top left*)
1st XI Football

(*left*)
1952 2nd XI Cricket...
2006, assets of £400
million +, for some!

(*above*)
Harrap, Palmer-
Tomkinson, NK, Bradbury

(*right*)
The losing finalist

Blackden Manor

Prime Minister Harold Macmillan
in the works

The old Kenyon headquarters in Bury

The Mill Girls

Wedding Mk 1

Wedding Mk 2

grace' was introduced in the form of Dancing Class. What at outset may sound rather sissy at such a young age has been nothing but a bonus all my life, to which I regularly refer and give the credits to Mum. Wednesday afternoons it was Miss Archbutts' academy in Altrincham. No ring-a-roses here, but straight into basic ballroom steps – quickstep, waltz, polka, samba and team dances, even an eight-some reel. I quickly took to these and they have provided a platform for fun, possibly tainted on certain occasions by exhibitionism. The closer clinch moments of ear-whispering 'don't you dance nicely, Nigel', followed by even closer body contact, have always paid dividends… thank you, Mum!

On January 20th 1949 – my eighth birthday – I was standing in the drive of my preparatory school Cothill House, near Abingdon. First biig mistake, parents. Being under 8 the previous September it was decided that I should wait a term, and consequently was out of the year's flow. What difference did three months make, particularly off the base of the highly focused one-on-one teaching one had up till then? James Pike, the headmaster's nephew and a year ahead, announced that he was my 'father' for an introductory period, and away we went.

Cothill, with about one hundred pupils, had the most wonderful layout. [r2] Surrounded by real countryside, yet only ten minutes south of Oxford, it was ideally situated for communications and other schools for competition. Facilities were kept in tip-top condition as the headmaster was very games oriented, as well as enthusiastic for hobbies and pastimes. He always wanted boys to be occupied… and who would not be with individual pitches for cricket only – the top pitch still has a little thatched pavilion – and soccer pitches doubling for field hockey in the Easter term. A charming nine-hole golf course with holes ranging from 60 to 220 yards, and where the boys took a part in helping maintain greens and bunkers, alongside four grass tennis courts, completed the outdoor picture.

A .22 25-yd rifle-range had been established in the redundant air raid shelter. A five-round 'possible' with no rest and real rifles at 12 years old... no problem for several of us. (Sad to note that in the twenty-first century a ban on even adult rifle clubs forces our GB Olympic rifle teams downwards to rehearse their shooting overseas.)

A fine old-fashioned gymnasium also included boxing. The 8-year-olds went in like tigers, occasionally to the screams of mothers on sports days when tempers were lost and a free-for-all ensued, which even the master in charge as referee found hard to disentangle! A squash court was a great start for us future rackets players.

The swimming pool was a large, homemade, outdoor affair, with very suspect filtration and no heating... dark pea (pee?) green water was the usual. A far cry from modern-day middle England models in Alderley Edge or at their Majorcan veeya alternatives.

Natural history was supported by a very extensive marsh, absolutely bulging with flora and fauna. This provided limitless field-craft opportunities, but only strictly supervised. The 'marsh' was the real thing, and livestock had been known to sink without trace in certain spots.

Indoor activities included a workshop, a stamp collecting club and a fine little library which was maintained daily by the boys. Newspapers were provided and never to my knowledge edited, which might be rather different today. News sometimes included commercial, political or social scandals which had befallen luckless parents, read about avidly and discussed in great detail by their offspring... modern paparazzi would have had a field day!

The boys ranged from aristocrats – when I first went there was a plethora of 'titles' ranging from a Marquess down to mere Hons – an Indian prince who turned up for a spell whilst his father did his Oxford bit, sons of old-established/newer model landowners and industrialists, and then the professional mix of clergy, academia and

City progeny… all long on gut. This produced natural ability which was encouraged to flourish.

Classroom started for me in the 'governess' form, with Miss Wright – known by 8-year-olds upwards as 'wagglebum' due to the size of her posterior – a kindly soul, and acted as an assessment filter to place boys in appropriate forms. The system allowed for no holding back for exceptional ability. Thus a bilingual pupil in French could be placed into the top French form, and yet still languish in a lower structure for the rest of his weekly intake. The balance of the school teaching was by masters, some married, with bachelors very carefully selected, no light loafers recruited here. All had to have some other real talents to contribute, either for the games or recreation activities.

Latin was a basic for all, Greek for the specialists – thank goodness – French stuttered along (literally), and the others always seemed to be interesting. Science was non-existent and scripture was supposed to be wonderful because the local vicar took it. In actual fact the Revd Dennis was rather liberal, and merely told biblical stories which we suspected were rehearsals on a live audience for a forthcoming sermon. Sure enough there was always a lapse of a few weeks and there it was, often embroidered and read out; the ad lib versions were much better.

He also supplemented his income by invigilating at exams, usually reading a newspaper for the entire time. Did he spy through a pinprick hole? On my vital 'life or death' Common Entrance occasion I must confess to writing an exact copy of my neighbour's essay on some very obscure history subject. He was a 'genius', had finished the entire paper in twenty minutes, and I was of course aware that he was aiming at a different school when I flashed him the emergency signal. Dennis suddenly crashed his paper down, only to announce that he had to apologise for falling asleep and in fact time was up… the usual 'oh sir, just a few more minutes' was always granted.

Assembly in the morning and evening flew under the title Prayers and, apart from saying 'sum' (I am here), prayers and lessons were read. The latter were always by boys, which included all but the first year. The appropriate mounting block was ready for those barely breaking four feet never mind five, and even then the reader could not be seen over the top of the lectern. This was a great start for speaking in public as we were coached accordingly for diction and speed. Evenings included a hymn usually played by the music master, but on Tuesday by a substitute in the shape of a very eccentric classics master. His repertoire, played by ear, consisted of 'Onward Christian Soldiers' and 'The Church's One Foundation' – the first now sadly deleted from modern hymn books as being considered 'politically incorrect'!

Sunday church was in the local village – a walk of *c*.1 mile, and we provided a choir from our strong school singing group. This was well run by our proper music master, and the piano also featured quite strongly. Any other instruments were discouraged but, if insisted upon, outside teaching came in from Oxford… I suspect at vast expense. So that's how we 'studied' for the goal of passing the Common Entrance exam during a period of five years. Very occasionally somebody got a scholarship.

Organisation and admin was structured around six groups – Carthaginians, Gauls, Greeks, Parthians, Romans and Trojans… classical upbringing or a forerunner of the EU?! These also acted as a catalyst for competition such as cross-country running and general field and track athletics, when all age groups could compete and points were scored. Peer pressure was on hand if you let your group down.

In both team and individual games I quickly progressed as an all-rounder. This meant playing at least a year ahead of my own year, sometimes with some surprises – beating the favourite for the golf prize, two years older and twice my size, only to be beaten in the final by 'my father' from my first term. I gravitated to the first football and cricket elevens a year in advance, captaining the latter for my final year. These gamesy activities seemed to add extra momentum to my preference for a properly organised show and I was elected head of the school for my last year.

Main ingredient for a successful school – the head, happily married for preference. For children, 'whether Buckingham Palace or Balham (US the Bronx) it all depends on home.' The combination produces the product which is set on a life pattern by 12. Leopards never change their spots, they just get bigger as they get older.

All was set for the next stage, preceded by another biig parental mistake. I had been asked, aged 11, whether I would like to try for Eton or Charterhouse, putting me in an awkward spot. Grandfather, his brothers and their subsequent offspring had all been at Eton, whilst my father and his two brothers had been sidetracked to Charterhouse due to a bad health record at Eton at the time. He always spoke highly of it, seemed to have enjoyed it, so I considered it diplomatic to plump for Charterhouse.

I had overlooked two important points. Cothill was a feeder for Eton and I was destined to lose contact with friends and their support. Secondly Charterhouse was probably the most demanding for the Common Entrance exams at the time and it meant passing into the school at a lower level... if anyone had bothered to consider this, how the hell was I to know? This was not helped by having to miss the first three weeks of the exam term due to having to be quarantined for my brother's scarlet fever. Work suffered, cricket went nowhere, and so it was at a reasonable level only that I was able to pass into a very differ-ent environment for the start of the second half of my boarding school career... or something like that!

3 Educating Nigel – Phase 2

'In skating over thin ice, our safety is in our speed' (Emerson)

By September 1954 Charterhouse was in the doldrums, i.e. a dump! One could possibly say a casualty of both World Wars. Having moved as a school from its original 1611 foundation site in London (now known as Old Charterhouse, in wonderful condition and housing sixty gentlemen (The Brothers) who have fallen on hard times and are predominately OCs) to Godalming in 1872, by the turn of the century upgrades were needed. Houses had been strung out either side of a valley leading into Godalming itself with the main part of the school focused on a neo-Gothic complex of cloisters, chapel and classrooms to match. The saving grace of this Victorian monster was the wonderful country locality, providing space galore for pitches and outdoor activities, which still holds good today. The First World War intervened, and similarly in the later 1930s, after the country had recovered from this and economic slump of unknown proportions, plans were once again put on hold on account of the Second World War. Consequently the structure of the school had hardly changed since 1872, with the exception of the introduction of electrics and the magnificent Gilbert Scott 'Memorial Chapel' – lest we forget. [b4]

So there I was standing at the new hops tea party with apprehensive parents and five other boys who I could instinctively tell were going to take a little getting to know, never mind become lifetime friends. Junior boys' 'cubes' were again not very encouraging. Iron frame beds were complemented by a stone floor and a tiny mat. The double doors at the end went out into the garden and did not close properly. Sash windows were nailed open and my father noticed that the blankets, of which there were two, were the same as when he had been there some thirty years earlier. (They happened to be a by-product at the 'Mill' so the next quarter I was able to at least keep warm.) Washing was in a tin basin which sat on a small cupboard and water was from a tap which was, of course, running stone cold by the time the juniors got their turn. The evening wash froze overnight.

The next floor up was the same for the more senior boys and the top three slept in one overcrowded room. Daytime one shared a 'carrol', an open space cubicle with a light over the top and a blank wooden half wall in front. This lasted for two years, when you graduated to a shared study room. This miserable state of affairs was reflected by the forthright Jewish American mother of a contemporary friend in another house: 'gee, and what does yourr Darrtmoorr look like!'

My first 'quarter' (although we ran on three normal terms, quarters had the prefix Oration, Long and Cricket, tying for first place lunacy with the Eton 'half') was a period of readjustment. One was at the bottom of the heap and vulnerable. There were two weeks to learn the ropes with tests in front of senior boys to see if you had passed, nothing untoward but then you were in the 'system'. Fagging – running errands, tasks such as cleaning shoes for monitors, sweeping out rooms – was the norm for the first year and disciplining within the house was by boys. The latter could escalate to a pitch whereby the cane could be administered, with permission from the housemaster, boy on boy.

This tradition was quite absurd and we took good care to see that it did not happen when my turn came at the top of the pile. Both fagging and corporal punishment have been taken out of the school system as a whole years ago and quite right too. I must add that throughout my educational 'career' I was never on the receiving end from either boy or master. It's what's called careful planning, moving swiftly over the ice, keeping in the long grass!

The work front looked dicey. I had moved into the lower half of the school but, after early assessment of the previous year's duds and the new hops, it looked as though one could get a first term 'promo' and get back on stream for natural progression to O- and ultimately A-level standards. One big drawback, the 'hash beak' (form master) was also new and hadn't a clue. He was in his early twenties with Harrow, National Service and some shaky University degree behind him. His discipline was almost nil and academically he was obviously hopeless, but basically a nice fellow and a games player which is where I got on with him a lot better. (He stayed at Charterhouse as a bachelor beak for the rest of his life.) I missed the promotion by two places in the cut-off and this consigned me to the slow lane.

The beaks generally were on a par with the school. Out of fifty or so there were about half a dozen who made sense and seemed normal. The rest were hangovers from the past and very much pre-war, often seemingly tired of the whole idea, bitter and even resentful. One form master later in my stay openly denounced the public school system in front of the whole form, and he was a housemaster.

Our own housemaster, although couth enough, was again entirely unsuitable, being an eccentric bachelor of the 'classics and beat 'em' variety. He was seriously crippled with arthritis, which he bore all his life with amazing courage, and hid behind his old cricket club ties. [b5] He was also an Old Carthusian, and his very sharp brain enabled him to remember minute detail about everybody in both the cricketing world, where he'd played at occasional county level, and every OC that ever lived. (I am absolutely certain that all housemasters and housemistresses – Eton recently leading the way here with a housemistress in a boys' school – must be happily married with the opposite number taking a close supporting role. This is now mandatory in nearly all GB boarding schools.) He spent the holidays sponging off smarter parents and old friends, or boring the pants off all in the Long Room at Lord's Cricket Ground. As a games player, particularly rackets, and son of a contemporary OC I was well in; he just needed diplomacy. This was another skill which was quickly developed in this human melange and, having left the school, I was immediately promoted to the inner circle. 'Nigel, you're far too civilised to continue calling me sir, do call me Bob.' Recognition indeed!

Over all this team the 'captain' was the most sinister. Young by name, and also at the time when he took over aged 30 in 1952, it was obvious that this egomaniac was going to milk the system for all it was worth on behalf of himself. The older beaks loathed him, and maybe with good reason. He was usually dressed in dark suits, a black gown, strutting around with his hands behind his back... what a farce. The headmaster's once-a-quarter sermon was set up on a plane equivalent to the then Archbishop of Canterbury who, as our senior governor, also used to perform... both breathtakingly arrogant. As a Cambridge hurdling blue we never saw him in a tracksuit helping with coaching although the athletics track was twenty yards from his new 'headman's house', built to distance the headmaster from running an actual school house. He played fives with the boys occasionally, never showed up anywhere near the corps (surely 1941/5 RNVR in destroyers had something to pass on) like the other masters, who coyly put on Second World War or National Service uniform and propped it up. His pretty wife Fiona obviously kept this masquerade as far from her daily life as she dared, sometime flying what we interpreted as distress signals wrapped in a most charming smile. This could be supplemented with a 'hello', plus, when you were in recognition, yes, your Christian name, euphoria! It was reported that a very attractive monitor planned to make a pass at her... I wonder if he succeeded! (Boys have very good noses, and don't forget it's the 'head' what makes the place, as per the last chapter.)

But behind this was something more deeply rooted when a principal obviously gunned for boys from the old guard backgrounds. Maybe it was the scholarship boy aspect (Eton & King's Cambridge) followed by five years' Eton teaching which switched on that chippy, I'll show 'em approach. Wonderful grounding however for honing the volume knob for later... maybe the 'greatest of these is Jealousy'.

A report on yours truly, 'This boy is too worldly-wise.' Surely that's what we were meant to be finding out?! The real classic came from another from the same stable – he mid-twenties, an old Wykehamist, me 16. 'Without straining himself unduly he has worked adequately in all these subjects. He shines at English, but with rather a lurid light: the opinions he utters in his essays on current topics are distasefully [actual typo] intolerant at the expense of argument. I hope he will come to regard the human race as less uniformly damnable than he seems to do now.' Maybe, supported by close reading, exposure and basic instinct, I had already spotted the change of direction of GB politically and socially, the flattening of the 'pyramid'. However, it would have been unfair to bet on who was going to get more fun out of life... and already these fellows knew it!

Individual games such as squash, fives and rackets featured strongly and I ran the rackets for my last year. After school colts level, cricket faded to the side which toured local villages on bicycles. This nearly came to serious grief when there was a mass pile-up on a return journey, suitably primed with bitter. A very pompous old colonel type who had nearly driven through the lot demanded which school we came from. Cranleigh School, being just down the road, got the blame and no more was heard.

My last year was just great. I was able to unofficially drive myself to the school, I had a girlfriend who was studying at Oxford and occasionally managed to mastermind trips to see her, or just get to London for cinema and days out. A tame taxi driver on the Godalming station rank was a close collaborator; he had the away rackets matches contract! The great incentive was not to get caught, particularly with the unpleasant attitude around in the masters' camp.

Several contemporaries have kept up as friends, noticeably those who were 'individuals' and have gone on to be successful under their own steam. We have not all become secretaries to golf clubs, which seems to be the cry of one member of house who, although beating us to a knighthood by sitting closely on the political splice whilst consecutive editor of two national dailies, was always considered an 'etcetera' when it came to the games department. Perhaps this is the cause of his aggression towards 'games players', whilst hopefully garnering invitations for the less obvious fields of shooting and fishing through articles written mainly about himself. His extensive countryside knowledge however provides an ideal backdrop for his current position as chairman of the CPRE (Council for Protection of Rural England)... is there any left?!

This school chapter could ramble on (the holidays feature in following appropriate places), but I want to end it with a story (a reprint of mine on the back of recent obituaries) which emanated from confirmation class under the tutelage of a certain Revd Jack Rutherford. This Bentley-driving padre was a real special. The other main character, Kit, was a study-mate, whose father had been murdered by the Japanese. This left his mother in straitened circumstances, but Kit was always determined not to let his family down.

Five of us Bodeites were due to be confirmed in LQ 1957. Class for this occasion meant a 9 pm trudge across the valley from the old house to the fireside comfort of Jack's house, where scripture was based on discussion of life generally, primed by the sherry decanter which was always offered on arrival. During one of our sessions Jack suddenly announced how he'd been able to help Kit's father during internment and had been with him when he died. We were on the edge of our seats, all ears, extending to utter amazement when handsome photograph albums were produced, depicting scenes which made some of the most unpleasant bits in the film 'Bridge on the River Kwai' look very mild. It transpired that Jack was an expert photographer, and the pictures had been smuggled out of the camp and published in the Times. A camera had been constructed using old tins and spectacle lenses. When questioned as to how film had been found, Jack told his confirmands that in certain cases the commandments had to be shelved, in this case 'thou shalt not steal'. I am sure that he never put anyone at the risk of certain execution, if discovered, other than himself.

Oh that the rest of Brooke Hall had matched up to this fine example and the other 'half dozen or so'. I am pleased to report that all the old houses were pulled down years ago and re-sited, allowing all students to have their own bed-sits. Charterhouse in 2006 [r3] is currently on the crest of a glorious wave, and they are queuing up for Cothill.

4 *Commerce*

'Among those dark satanic mills' (Blake)

Let's start by putting the summary first and consider where the dosh, moolah, long green stuff, lucre or whatever comes from. Quite simply you legally can: (a) officially inherit it, (b) receive it as a gift, (c) marry it, or (d) earn it. Following the lines of a popular TV game show, *Who Wants to Be a Millionaire*, take away two of the wrong answers (a and c in this case) and I will declare a draw on the remaining two for meaningful contribution… supported by good luck and graft!

I never really considered anything other than going into the 'Mill'. Literally centuries of existence had built in a gut atmosphere which spread through all who worked there. There was a sense of loyalty that demanded two-way respect between employees and employers, we were all in it together. The company had moved into a Ltd. shareholding amongst the family from sole proprietorship in 1907, to go public in 1947 (wrongly structured) as a hindsight measure after the Second World War . 'Look what might have happened if Uncle had died'… well he hadn't! Great-uncle Myles, having captained Lancashire cricket in the early 1920s, put himself forward as chairman of the company on the death of his father in 1924 with a salary of £7,500 p.a., watered down by the family from his suggestion of £10,000. He promoted managers to run the business and promptly bought a house near Stow-on-the-Wold in Gloucestershire, with its own cricket ground… quite a long way from Bury!

By 1959 there were four mills which manufactured industrial and commercial fabrics. These divided 50/50 wool and cotton based, with similar style manufacturing techniques on basic natural fibres for ever being superseded and blended with synthetics. The two woollen mills – vertical manufacturing from raw fibre and a wet finishing plant – focused attention on felts for the papermaking industry, with laundry machinery clothing and other industrial cloths as runners-up. Due to being more sophisticated fabrics, this division was the heavyweight of the group in both turnover and profitability terms.

The two cotton mills, again one vertical and a special weaving plant, concentrated on filter cloths for all types of substance and air filtration, supported by commercial covers for lorries and ships, and standard cotton sheeting. No ordinary 'domestics' these, such as clothing, carpets, furnishings which merely happen after they leave your factory. Not only did industrials go through anything up to thirty different processes to meet exact, yes 100% specification, but one had to know how they were used and be able to talk knowledgeably to customers and agents from both sides of the table. On top of this there was basic business – sales, production, admin – to be learned. I always include finance in admin. So… fast learning curve required, as it was presumed that as a member of the family one knew it anyway.

This required practical apprenticeship-style training in t'Mill. Literally starting at the bottom I was to spend six months in the wool buyer's office to learn about our raw materials, and get a general grasp as to how they were applied and worked up the various processes to fabric 'in the grease', i.e. before finishing. The next stage was off to

Canada to actually work in the mills of a friendly competitor on the machinery itself.

On the first Monday of October 1959, 7.30 a.m. (no silly years off to get into trouble) I was standing in the wool buyer's office feeling spare. 'Don't just stand there, lad, take yer coat off' thawed the ice, and I immediately felt more at ease. (This is a Lancastrian trait... thoroughly decent people, simple as that. Yorkshire folk are more reserved: take the visiting cricketing team: 'when we comes 'ere we say 'ow do, and we don't say owt till we says 'owzat.')

Norman immediately had me into a brown mill overall 'which we always wear in t'Mill' and round we went. It was not exactly virgin territory. Days during school holidays had been spent for a general look-see and I had given a lecture at Charterhouse on how to make a paper machine felt, much to the astonishment of the so-called economics beak and his experimental economics form – what did a nice retired naval commander know about economics anyway?

Our first tea break together introduced me to the *Telegraph* cryptic crossword and I have been a fan of crosswords generally ever since. Books had to be kept, and my ally's meticulous prize-winning script coupled with his electric mental maths calculations made my scrawl and no O-level maths standard look very poor. This cemented our team even further.

Wednesday was the turn of the wool and synthetic fibre salesmen from Yorkshire to visit the industrial fabric manufacturers in Lancashire... same fibres but different products as compared with their traditional wool and worsted cloth producers 'over t'top'. Smaller, specialist suppliers were often represented by the principal of the firm and included such names as Cullingworth, Ackroyd, Mitchell and Bottomley. Jokes, ciggies and general intelligence about competitors, entwined with review of samples and hard bargaining over price, were the order of each visit, sometime with complaints or review of stock involving our head sorter and wool foreman – Charlie

Warburton and Billy Rothwell. The latter was a regular daily visitor, putting my maths ability even further into the shade by going through his modest horse racing investments for the day, such as twists, doubles and yankees – all to be collected by the bookies' runner who stood at the main gate when the 12 o'clock siren went for lunch.

Our wool office also paid reciprocal visits to Yorkshire to see the tykes on their home turf, maybe play them at golf, and I once suggested that we host a dinner in the evening. (We were staying anyway. A journey over the Pennines that takes forty minutes today could take anything up to four hours on the old roads, with fog, ice and snow to match.) This was a great success, but the following day I had a memorable interview with one of the real old men of wool, sitting on a fleece which draped his high-back chair, and dressed in immaculate herringbone worsted with highly polished handmade brown brogue shoes.

(In your best Yorkshire) 'Well, Nigel lad, we're all very pleased over 'ere in Bradford that you've joined the firm. Kenyon's is one of the great family names in business; but if an old man can give you a bit of advice, beware of all Jews and Catholics. We've got some over 'ere now in t'trade and they're buggers.' Oh well, couldn't agree on that one, as we had good social friends and business allies in both camps… lucky he hadn't expounded his views to my erstwhile beaks at Charterhouse. Talk about two ends of the spectrum. He died soon afterwards leaving several millions, and just in time not to see the first mosque in GB which must be in walking distance of his long-gone warehouse premises.

Due to early starts, proper fog and non-existent motorways, I took digs on the north side of Bury, an old farmhouse bordering on the bleak start of North Lancashire countryside. My landlady was an eccentric, but great fun for all of that. 'I don't do any cleaning [and that included the bath!], smoke [like two chimneys] and evening time

I like a cocktail… I hope you're not teetotal.' She forgot to mention the damp. On the plus side she was a marvellous cook, a seamstress and we had kindred spirit conversation. Her husband just beamed. My evening cape – at material cost only, made from the finest barathea, silk-lined and initialled – is still going strong and always attracting green-eyed compliments.

March 1960 and I was off to Canada for six months. With luggage way in excess of flying allowance, I was booked onto the Cunard Line *Corinthia*, Liverpool to Montreal. Our Liverpool friends and cotton brokers knew the line well to the extent that I was enrolled as the VIP passenger… rather to the chagrin of some very senior Canadians and Brits, but possibly this was also a safety measure for the captain to keep an eye on me. Well, he certainly did! Immediately foreseeing a real boring six days coming up for a young adventurer he gave me 'freedom of the ship'… much to the amazement of the seasoned cabin staff. This enabled one to pass the very strictly controlled barriers between the first and cabin classes, and so with my dinner jacket full of the finest dinner and wines to match, I headed for the ballroom at the back. The band, Sid Phillips dance/Dixie style, stimulated some energetic jiving, lots of flying skirts and pretty emigrating Irish legs. Third day out, the ship was tossing like a cork. My steward appeared: 'Don't move, sir, just take this and I'll call you for lunch.' I passed out and wakened for a hearty lunch with only a handful of other people in the entire dining room. The fourth day we stopped in fog which, on clearing, revealed icebergs. The last night I won the five-day roll-up bingo prize, enabling me to lavishly entertain my friend(s) in the 'back' and leave the ship distributing largesse in rather an inflated fashion, particularly to my steward with the blue pills.

I was met by Tom Milnes, the managing director of my host company, in his blue Cadillac, smoking a cigar and accompanied by his attractive second wife. He got a big kick out of this, as some forty years earlier he had been recruited as a mill hand from our finishing mill in Bury, and emigrated to become the head of one of our friendly competitors. His obvious Lancashire accent laced with Canadian/US expressions was very charming, but that fine Lancastrian welcoming quality hadn't been lost.

Ayers Ltd. in Lachute was situated some 40 miles north of Montreal at the start of the Laurentian Mountains. The layout had all the usual ingredients of a one-street mill town, with the mills situated down by the river for the finishing element of woollen cloth. My living quarters were a suite in a new motel which had been built in conjunction with a new championship style golf course with club house to match... literally across the road. They were absorbing the bill on my behalf and I was left to solve my transport question. It so happened that the one and only dealer had a low-mileage 100/6 Austin Healey sports right there, so on a guaranteed deal – which in fact showed me a profit at the end of my visit – I was mobile!

I started in t'mill in the card room (combing out fibres to eliminate all the rubbish and at the same time create a lap for the next stage of spinning) and my colleagues on the shop floor were French Canadians. Now this species is not Canadian or French, but a swarthy Teutonic mixture, sometimes with a good dose of Red Indian thrown in. Ordinary French language gets by and provided for some ice-breaking mirth. But they were waiting for me to pass the test.

I was given the task to 'fettle' a card. (Clean out the serious pile/counter-pile wire rollers with aid of a curry comb, suitably clad in leather knee and elbow pads for protection whilst scrambling over the rolls anything up to fifteen feet in the air.) All was going well, but I gradually noticed an increasing amount of bony looking pieces coming out on my comb... to the accompaniment of much giggling in the corner. It transpired that an unfortunate hand had got his arm shaved off (as the wire can do instantaneously as it drags you in) the day before! These were tough guys right enough, but I passed and thereafter they always helped 'le jeune anglais', which must be growled in the back of your throat blended with liberal pine tar from seriously revolting cigarettes.

I was not on the payroll as such, but Tom always came round on Fridays and presented me with a brown wage packet containing $50 Canadian. This gave him a feeling of being back in Lancashire when he'd been on the receiving end. He had, of course, been there in the early part of the twentieth century, so I got first-hand stories and information not only about my family but also the mill and conditions of the time. It was very obvious that he had expanded Ayers on our Kenyon lines. Staffed crèches for the mill girls' infants, canteens with subsidised lunch, outside healthcare support, ex-gratia pensions from the company in recognition of long service... it's called sharing!

Late May, and I was to join the company plane, with directors and managers, to go down to Atlantic City for the world textile machinery show, and 'don't forget your dinner jacket'. The Convention Hall was a real eye-opener: vast, and packed with every kind of textile machine, often all running at prescribed times. (The Japs were sitting noticeably beside exhibits... sketching away with great big grins on their faces... not very popular.) Ayers hosted a black tie dinner in our hotel where I was introduced and spoke briefly. Afterwards, at the invitation of a Swiss loom maker, who had their eyes on our business back home, we repaired to 'Ricky's Hileah Club'.

This was a show club with all the trimmings, up from the south for the summer season, superb band and predominately black showgirls to match. The cabaret sizzled and they had me up on the stage to join the dancing and even sing. Our party faded away, and I was left with the invitation from my Swiss host to continue as long as I liked – 'we are all paid up.' The evening ended with me escorting two of the girls home, and then tucking into an early breakfast back at our hotel... only to be surprised by one of the directors: 'morning, Nigel, the plane leaves at ten.'

I continued back at the mill in various manufacturing departments, but decided to follow my father's suggestion that I spend some time in the US, particularly as mills tended to close up for the months of July and August. Two more early autumn months of mill graft followed, and I closed my first transatlantic adventure by taking the sleeper from Montreal to New York (fine old black stewards, club cars, the lot) and sailing back in the *QE1*.

This was one of her last journeys, not very full, but made pleasant by being asked up to the Cockpit Club for dinner on the second night and the rest of the trip by a good-looking mother on behalf of her pretty daughter. Just the three of us, but mum was watching me very closely and offspring was always whisked away to bed under close escort. One evening, being left on my own, I plucked up courage and asked actress Vivien Leigh, also on her own, to dance. She was travelling with a toy boy who seemed to be getting the heave-ho, as confirmed by them leaving the ship early at Southampton, to avoid the popping flashbulbs and newshounds. 'How sweet of you [patting my arm] but I think probably better not tonight.'

So it was back to Bury, my farmhouse digs and more practical experience in t'Mill. However, my Canadian trip had not only given me some practical knowledge as to running textile machines but also a very close look as to how a competitor – and a very well-organised one at that – worked. Simple truth of the matter, the goose (JK&S) that had laid the golden eggs, silver spoons, or whatever, was dying. My brief experience told me that our management procedures and financial controls were virtually non-existent, our machinery was seriously dated, particularly when considering a new process of making felts, aka 'needling'. This would require massive capital expenditure to even remain in the market at all. Woollen mule spinning, and non-automatic looms on the lighter side, were just the other runners – progressing backwards.

And where was I to go with all this? The senior structure of the company was top-heavy with family and faithful old managers who were accommodated on a 'job with us is a job for life' principle, whilst the lower ranks were closing fast. This included the sales team who were well managed, selling top-class products backed by a first-class name and exporting over 40% of our output... supported by excellent agents, often of many years' standing. Exports had always been a must-have on the agenda. In certain camps we'd go on for ever, never mind three hundred years!

I was enrolled at the Anne Shaw Organisation on a serious business course. The principal had not only been in industry herself, but had learnt her management techniques trade at the knee of Professor J. K. Galbraith, a pioneer of industrial engineering, who is still referred to today, and who featured on grainy black and white films in our classes. (Recently deceased aged 97, this Canadian-born American blowhard dismissed views with which he frequently disagreed under the cover of 'the conventional wisdom shows us that...' Conversely he was one of the few prominent Americans to emerge with credit from an interview with the satirist Ali G.)

The focus of the three months' course, lectured by her senior consultants, was intensive study of industrial engineering such as O&M, works' costings, product mix... you name it, run alongside a practical project from your own company. My five other classmates were senior managers from major manufacturing concerns, so one had an added bonus by being able to learn by example from significantly older people and their experience. They were billeted in a local hotel – I was able to commute 8 miles from home – and we joined up after hours for unwind and some fun. One student was particularly taken with mine host's wife, and I was seriously attracted to a voluptuous Scandinavian who was helping in the hotel on an exchange management scheme. (Combining business with pleasure... or as the Dachshund said to the Alsatian, 'it's been a business doing pleasure with you.')

The mill was obviously wide open for management development and so on my return I proposed that we create a development department. But this needed an experienced head, not just a junior and a member of the family at that. Answer: I recruited one of Anne Shaw's best consultants… for which she never forgave me, to the extent of no speakums when I found myself sitting next to her on a domestic flight sometime later. John was just a great colleague, friend and my own private business tutor. He had extensive experience in industry as a senior consultant, and possibly even learnt something from us. He went on to retirement, after Bury and head of the world-class consulting group Hay-Msl.

This new office gave me the key to get involved in every aspect of the company alongside specific projects for overall improvement. Departments were realigned and trimmed, machinery was scrapped to be replaced with huge cost benefits in capacity and wage savings, a mill was sold off, sheds were refurbished for general efficiency, Victorian coal-fired boilers were replaced with oil, new methods were adopted in manufacturing procedures and work flow, and that was just in t'Mill. I also had attended a financial course on 'company finance' – capital, balance sheets, public company structure, and the rest. Not 'I've got an MBA' and therefore know how to run a business, accompanied by classroom clichés to blind you with mystery. Just practical, down-to-earth understanding… sort of common sense, even for a lad with no O-level maths!

A proper finance director was hired and again the cracks were confirmed as reality. Our recruit had a particular understanding of insurance, and this led to a complete overhaul of not only the overall company insurances, saving thousands of pounds in premium, but also the pensions. Some members of the family had not even got one. Our new broker also introduced me to the structure of Lloyd's Underwriters and how one could join in as an outsider… luckily I did not have the necessary to enrol!

We acquired and closed a smaller competitor all to our advantage, but a new venture for us, called budgeting and forecasting, was showing up an amber light: we were going to start losing money. A derisory offer for the company had been made by a British competitor, but I encouraged the board to let me sound out an American company who I had called on previously. In short, a deal was done, late autumn 1968. A good consolation prize for shareholders, sighs of relief from members of the family outside the company, and also senior members still in who were due to retire anyway. But what happens to the tenth generation, just my brother and me? A rump end holding of a few shares and 'we'll need you fellas'… oh yeah!

January 1969 I was to be shipped over to the Albany Felt Co. Inc. to 'see how we do things' for three months, obviously to get me out of the way whilst fast and furious changes were made in Bury. However, I had one big trump card in my pocket. Prior to going I had heard, through the wall in the next door office, an Albany executive – the acquisitions vp who had worked with me on the deal – confiding to a senior member of the family, 'Of course we shall be getting rid of him at the end of the period' – what a coup. I told no one till the end of the visit… and it was going to cost 'em!

I was installed in the Fort Orange Club at the back of the State Buildings: an old-fashioned men's club built c.1810 with late Victorian and Edwardian additions. Squash courts, a fine old pool and steam room were bonuses, and in the evenings I virtually had the whole place to myself after sports and supper had finished. The latter could be with various state senators who stayed in the week (New York City is not the state capital) or sometimes with the only other resident, a delightful retired US general with whom I re-lived various battles, he using the table condiments and silverware as props. 'Patton was here'… etc. He was also very up on the Vietnam situation, raging away at the time. 'Sad to say our boys are over-equipped, under-trained and very poorly commanded.' (The Green Berets and the 101st Airborne were, and still are, the exceptions, as recounted later by veterans of the whole affair.)

Being a 'men only' club (it still is today but registered in the directory under, er, 'nightclubs') there wasn't sight of a female with the exception of an outstanding Brigitte Bardot lookalike who served in the dining room... she lived in a flat at the back.

The company assistant personnel manager, who also edited the company newspaper, was a startlingly good-looking Irish-American redhead. Not so long after my arrival I found a note hidden in my blotter suggesting that we made a date to go out shortly, but in no way was I to tell anyone and she would trust me to comply. It transpired that prior to my arrival a memo had been sent round the office 'forbidding' any female employees to 'date' your author. (Sounded like Dad laying down the law. 'No dating girls in the office, the mill or indeed in Bury.') It's called shxxting on your own doorstep, except Albany was not my doorstep. On a no strings attached basis we had a good time, although her job was at risk. For transport a '5 litre Ford Mustang' sedan had been hired for me, which was just fine for trips at weekends to New York, Tuxedo Park and the surrounds. An unusual speeding incident will be elaborated on later.

The work side of things was mundane routine, deliberately to brass me off, but I made it my business to get on with all the lower ranks in the office and in the mill. They loved it, the senior management did not, but I knew something they thought I didn't. I also spent time on away trips with the salesmen, which often lasted a whole week, and took in more remote locations around the paper mills. Air stewardesses were selected in those days for looks and personality and it showed. I was a novelty as an ally, the sales lads knew the social ground at our various destinations, and away we went... shades of Atlantic City! [b6]

But the end was near and I was summoned to the president's office to be told that I could either be a salesman or leave the company with one month's salary. I was able to smile benignly and advised him to reconvene our meeting for midday Friday. I told him about my prior knowledge of the plot, I was going to send him a memo outlining a serious severance package, and that he'd better read it carefully. The 'otherwise' bit mentioned such words as press, exposure of his senior executive plotter and a scene to match back at Bury on my return. Due notice was taken, I was paid up in multiple £000s, and they were to pick up all my expenses in the US over the duration of my stay; the meter had been running. I tried to pull a finder's fee for my part in orchestrating the deal to which the answer was 'No... but there's quite a bit more to you than I thought' – with which we parted on good terms.

I immediately returned to Bury – via NYC – and left the company, never to return. My brother Donald took away a piece of the light industrial division, which he turned into a success by diversifying into specialist sports ground covers for areas such as Wimbledon Tennis Club and Lord's Cricket Ground. This business has recently been sold, allowing him to retire. There is still a James Kenyon division in Bury, still part of the Albany Felt Co., which is one of only four main players left in the field of industrial fabrics.

I decided to take three months off: do up my house, enjoy the summer and find a job. The third easier said than done! The phone did not ring off the hook, senior family commercial contacts were zero, I answered advertisements, sent CVs, but suddenly I was lunched by a prominent financier.

'Now, Nigel, you're a bright young fellow, we've checked out your ability, and we think that we've got a business which you could become seriously involved with. We are prepared to match the required investment and back you.' This was more like it. 'Tell me more.' 'Well... [ten minutes]... and this would require you to come up with £50k, easily managed I'm sure from your share of the Kenyon sale.' I knew of the company: what an opportunity, but sadly a polite rejection… and I've never seen a bill come so quick.

But the phone rang again and I joined a small provincial merchant bank on the venture capital side of things, appraising and helping with start-up/second stage investments. This meant that I could bring my practical experience into play, which was a new one for the 'what's the PE ratio' accountant types. Our clients liked this approach and I enjoyed visiting them on a regular monthly basis. But this was obviously only short term and, after having a look at Australia and a year in the stock exchange as a clerk, I decided to start my own business. (There are three levels of individuals who invest themselves and their money in a new/established business, Mr A, Mr B and Mr C. A has nothing, even developed 'gut', B has a certain amount of capital, C has everything and more. A will borrow, gear up and go for it, not minding, if all fails, reverting back to being Mr A. Mr C can afford to drop the investment and still be Mr C. Mr B, however, will be much more hesitant in committing himself; he does not want to go backwards and become a Mr A.)

So, as a Mr B with a minimum of £000s and some gut, I opened a small office (don't work from home, even a stable across the yard is different from the kitchen table) in Knutsford in 1973 with an experienced private secretary to help.

Knutsford not only had the attraction of being an historic town from several different centuries, but also Iris, an elegant divorcee, who ran her own restaurant. This high quality watering hole was also on the list for the great American Anglophile, financier and philanthropist Paul Mellon. He would detour from Ireland, where he kept his European racehorse team in training, to Manchester – plus entourage and Bentley 200 miles down from London for transport – especially to go to Knutsford, have dinner and see Iris. Knowing her as well as I did, I was privy to, and indeed involved around, several stories of his visits. She kept any form of personal liaison with him admirably at bay, to the extent that everybody remained friends.

Kenyon Business Services – rather a contrast to the Mellon Banking Corp. – was going to be a financial services type business that would sell your business and then we would advise on where the money should be placed. This would require supporting management as we expanded, and operating in cahoots with other professional offices which were to be hand-picked and come through impeccable connections and references. It ended up as a business broking operation – that fascinating roller-coaster ride of feast or famine. This kept me going – sometimes only just, but at all times very much on my toes – for some thirty years. Nothing more satisfying than presenting the final success fee through the bank grill yourself... comparable to 'owned, trained and ridden' in horse racing parlance.

I say 'success fee', as it was something I learned from Sandy, a shrewd New Yorker, who started a similar operation at the same time specialising in transatlantic deals for UK companies. 'I have learnt the hard way not to start without a "working fee" agreed at the beginning.' How right he was. They always try to haircut you at the end, so at least make sure you're covered as you go along. I had a substantial client who died on me halfway through the deal, a large overseas hotel sale was nail biting when I discovered who the owner really was, several decided not to proceed, some buyers were merely researching the market. Why paper the walls with worthless files... we were better than 'no foal no fee!' Deal involvement ranged in value from £1 the day before the receiver, to $25 million.

So much for commerce; other business-related tales and experiences will surface in later chapters.

5 The Ladies

'Now Watson the fair sex is your department' (Doyle)

Before we plunge into this minefield let's establish the backdrop, at least according to the gospel of yours truly. Simply... all women 16 to 60, 18 to 80ish like sex, but it all depends how the matter is approached and executed. This is measured on a class scale ranging from the top end 'do you feel better now Charles?' to the lower echelons 'going at it like crazed weasels'.

Secondly I must emphasise that I have never had an intimate moment of any sexual nature with a man and have no desire to do so whatsoever; not my scene, full stop. This must be already obvious from various adventures in earlier chapters. The awareness of gay behaviour has been heightened over the past twenty years and so much the better for that; everyone knows where they stand. Nevertheless it is a minority (3%) group at the centre.

Having watched their emancipation over this period in both the US and the UK, I would suggest that there are some basics which would make for even smoother acceptance, and more workable relationships. Stick to people from a similar background, don't champion the cause – there isn't one – and no adopting children, please.

Our holidays from boarding school were sprinkled with events and parties which always included girls... early days this was a hangover from kindergarten. Tea parties and sandpits graduated to simple dance parties and outside activities such as tennis and horse riding. For the former one sometimes went to stay with a school friend and summer holidays away provided the added variety of meeting others.

Once, what looked like being a real drag, Granny sponsoring a family beach holiday at Westward Ho!, brightened up considerably with my first international friend, Virginia, a precocious 12-year-old daughter of a smart Italian family. Our respective Dads played single figure golf matches. Teenage years followed a similar pattern and Scottish holidays again provided for plenty of mixed company fun. Various, er, intimacies broadened scope with maturity!

On my return from Canada I was able to key into friends who were up at Oxford. This had the advantage of being around on a par with the older ones who had done National Service (I missed by six months) and at the same time not being tied to the college disciplines. Great dances were held at such venues as Blenheim Palace, once with my XK Jaguar sticking in a ploughed field on the return home – what was it doing there in the first place? On another occasion my friends left the window open for me to climb in, not forgetting to fill the basin under the point of entry which was reached by flying across the back alley, some four floors up. This was after negotiating a climb via a tomb and a spring up to the ledge of the adjacent church, inching one's way along... dressed in a white tie and opera cloak with howling gale to add to the fun – or madness!

Now the female form of any age group rarely passes the all-round test of 'attractive' dressed, half-dressed or completely undressed, but 'Miss Oxford' certainly did, with flying colours... a sophisticated,

Manchester Tennis and Racquet Club

Mixed doubles team – first serves

Fiji

Eze

Long Island –
worldwide
contender for
the over 70s

Fishers Island

(*top left*) Mink hunting

(*bottom left*)
The Pytchley Hunt

(*above*) Brass monkey

(*right*) We borrowed
the dog

(*below*) Dove shootin'

(*bottom right*)
NK and Edward
Ulmann

Boro Sovereign – Norman Williamson up – heads for the judge

...and Penelope (on left) collects her prize! (*Photos: Colin Turner*)

A salmon not a minnow

A bluefish not a salmon

'Proteus' rises from the sea

'Bramble'

'Rupert'

'Rosie'

'Petal'

intelligent gal who literally bubbled. The bubble burst when, dropping her off after a Sunday lunch, she looked back over the folded top of my car: 'Oh my god, here comes xxxxx', and she was off like a startled rabbit. This two-timed suitor, who not only married my friend but went on to become a TV celebrity, was back a day early! We had a catch-up years later… after their divorce.

Weekdays up north were quiet as compared with the buzz of the capital, but then we had Manchester. Theatres and concerts were on a par with London, but on a smaller scale, and only twenty minutes from my works' flat in Bury. The club element, however, was on a different level: stag nights with North Country comedians (the best), gambling (watch only, whilst a mixture of hard-bitten players played 'chemmy dooffer', 'blaackjaack' or 'roolette'), great bands, great cabaret.

Our group were all working in family businesses or professional offices, and were adopted by some of the Manchester 'fraternity' as a contrast to their entourages. This meant boxing nights and other promotions, moving on to one of the clubs later where it was all laid on… fighters, football and showbiz celebs. This included Manchester fashion-model girls, who said 'pardon', drank 'brandy and benny', and were just perfectly relaxed and enthusiastic – typically Lancastrian. One night one of our corner announced that he was going to Paris for the weekend to watch the England/France rugby match, and then join the French Foreign Legion. We were all astonished to learn the following Monday that he had! [b7]

On the other side of town Cheshire blended into Staffordshire on one side and Shropshire on the other. The first, economically founded on textiles, took in the rich Manchester suburbs such as Altrincham, Knutsford and Prestbury… the second, pottery things, and some fine countryside… the third, engineering stuff, and even more countryside. Estates were owned by the aristocracy of many generations, industrialists who had honed 'the gut' and become rather grand, in the nicest possible way, and others who just thought they were and were learning fast. One was asked to private dances, often being given for no particular reason, asked to shoot, joined up for skiing parties, moved in on some London action in the week.

London had to be set up around a business trip so the family kept back the London merchants and clearing houses as personal territory. Debutante parties were still orchestrated on proper qualifications and style, whilst the theatre content was balanced and fresh and the great entertainers were continually on tour. I was a member of the Blue Angel and 400 Clubs (strictly members only) and the Berkeley Hotel was a natural mecca. The bandleader was married to a relation by marriage, so the centre alcove table was a cert, as was the restaurant gossip. 'See Ava Gardner over there in the corner with her latest? Oh... er, any problems? No... except maybe for the kitchen night staff who get a request for two rare steaks and two pints of beer about 3 a.m.!' George certainly knew the detail. The whole dance-music and cabaret scene made today's disco contributions look second-rate – at best.

Before going into the marriage stakes let's consult the 'gospel'. There's always lots of good advice flying around. 'It's all give and take... give him the last piece of toast and he'll be happy at the office all day... take a good look at the mother-in-law, that's what you're saddled with thirty years hence.' Well-meaning stuff, to which no one pays any attention! Keep it simple, it's going to be a roaring success or a hopeless flop on a 50/50 base, but fundamentally both parties have to be in harmony (i.e. completely in tune with any extremes either way) over sex, religion, money and politics. Any order you like, but the last does feature in today's social climate.

Well, I thought I'd found her... Elizabeth. Attractive, sporty, gold medal cook, liked the country, family owned old-established West End business, friends in common (so much better than having common friends), and away we went. But help, Nigel's not going to become a Roman Catholic.

No he's not, with celibate priests and murky areas such as confessional boxes around. The service of Mass ('marse' in the best circles) is very similar to Anglican Holy Communion, which has been adapted as from the early 1980s to gradually blend in with the wishes of the Vatican element of the proposed European Union in its final form. [b8][b9]

Enter the prospective mother-in-law who had brought papacy to their family... and subsequently ruled the roost, with little reasoning and some hypocrisy. My father-in-law had a previous wife still alive when they had married. 'What happened to till death us do part?' 'Oh, the marriage was annulled' – well that's all right then.

On comes the pet family padre, the one that roves around the high-rollers, stays for Christmas, and says Marse in the garden if required. Two good Martinis and well into the dinner wine, 'well my boy I'm sure we can work this out, marriage is about... blah blah blah!' 'Fine,' says I, 'but I always like to hear both sides, the theory and the practical. Are you qualified to comment on the latter?' We witnessed a purple-faced explosion, and home he went.

We were going ahead and, after a setback when I nearly died, we were married in September 1964. As the out-laws were obviously not on side (although my father-in-law sent his daughter a thumping great diamond and pink sapphire clip as a present... 'and don't tell mother'), the reception was held in the garden at my parents' home in Cheshire. The convoy to the Crewe Register Office (real basic in a back street, quite a contrast) consisted of three sports cars and two high-powered saloons, with tops down in recognition of the glorious day and white ribbons on the bonnets. Bystanders and shoppers in Crewe and villages between cheered and we all honked our horns. Cake and champagne in the garden, chauffeur back to Crewe train, and on the dot of nine we were entering the Berkeley restaurant to

'Here Comes the Bride'. Honeymoon at the Cap Estel in Eze (in those days you had to have a reference from a previous customer before you could book in) and back... to be met by the blue envelope – the mother-in-law's broomstick. This was to be a twice-weekly feature which gnawed away at our marriage for nine months, causing strife in one simple word, and ultimate break-up.

During that period I took time out to undertake a world trip on behalf of the 'Mill' in recognition of our tercentenary. I was accompanying the regular overseas salesman who, due to illness at home, had to bale out early on at our first stop in India, having trawled through Pakistan. This left me on my own to handle the sales aspect as well as the diplomatic/PR side of things. A car with a chauffeur and his Persian lamb hat at my disposal in Bombay... my Indian agent leaving me in Hyderabad to attend a cousin's wedding in Bangalore – whilst I coped with a two-day visit to Hyderabad Asbestos, one of our most significant customers world-wide... a sixteen-hour train journey for 300 miles with Bhowani Junction style stations to match... elephants in the pulp mills... jackals sniffing under the shutters of my ground floor room... a beautiful European lady who was staying at the Saturday Club in Calcutta – purely platonic, bar a memorable snog in a rickshaw... dinners and lunches galore.

These were often given by our customers, once including a request for a turbaned string band to play (in your best Anglo-Punjabi) 'Happy Birthday for Mr Kenyon, from the mill of the Kenyon family, many congratulations sir.' The rest of the very upmarket Indian customers, in the wonderful old glass-domed Empire ballroom, looked so startled that I decided to reply to our extensive table and include the whole room... to great applause!

Next stop Hong Kong. The Mandarin Hotel had just opened and my junior executive suite upgrade was next door to Natalie Wood and her entourage. A smile in the lift and early morning swim sighting, round the pool on the roof one floor up, confirmed that she was drop dead attractive, full stop! Australia and New Zealand were covered in the same intensity, a short stay over in New York and home. Pre-punched Telex tapes were the speediest form of communication for the daily reports, for a trip which was minuted as an outstanding success.

Travelling for the Mill was always fun, and memorable trips included visits to Greece. This was a comparatively small market, but serviced by an ideal one-man-band agency. Their business hours also meant that the mornings were free, opening the way for a walk up the hill, onto the bus and out to the Astir Beach Club. One morning a swim out to a sunbathing raft turned out to be very rewarding… and she was staying in my hotel!

On another trip to Belgium, an evening with the Bishop of Ghent was a highlight. The pontiff entertained us with Bollinger champagne and cigars in magnificent surroundings. He had dressed for the occasion in his best pink water silk and a cross round his neck composed of pigeon egg-sized emeralds… very impressive and very comfortable digs!

We had rented a small house out in Cheshire, but the family pressure continued, demanding apologies, how wicked we all were, to an extreme where blood was thicker than water, or in this case me. A most unpleasant writ arrived, demanding instant divorce on every ground one could think of. This was very directly contested, resulting in me being able to divorce her after the then two-year digestion lapse. A most welcome call halfway through this period, announcing that she wished to remarry, completed the deal entirely in my favour… except could I change my colours and let her divorce me!

She hired a detective, not to watch me in flagrante delicto, but to come and take a statement that I had 'been guilty of adultery with a woman unknown'. This involved him coming to Manchester, yes in a shabby brown raincoat from Brighton, so I gave him a slap-up lunch in the Midland Hotel with friendly waiters primed to complete the show. He gave me an interesting insight into how his seamy side of posh divorces worked and I poured him back onto the train. This gesture opened the door for a full fig white wedding à la Nuptial Marse with two hundred guests and our son, Philip, in attendance as a page... oh well. The latter had come on the scene rather by chance, I'm so glad that he did.

During the estrangement period we were both attending the wedding of a great friend in the castle home of her husband, where they still live today. The party really rocked as usual in this venue and, encouraged by a great bachelor funster friend of mine (who eventually got round to marriage aged 69: 'Why such a long wait, David?' 'Oh, I've been interviewing for fifty years.'), my proposition to join me for the night in The Crown at Stone was accepted... we were technically still married!

I ultimately bought the house, but the 'golden goose' had stopped laying eggs and the main gap opening up was transport. The following chapter within the chapter will condense fifty years of motoring into one.

☞

We soon became aware of cars from a background of a car-owning family and good ones at that. This was also prompted by an uncle who had raced at Brooklands, Le Mans and elsewhere in privately entered teams of Aston Martins and others. Early on in the piece there was an edict 'there will be no motor bikes or any motor racing'. To compensate for this enthusiasm and to prevent any trials out onto the open road, a 1932 Austin 7 was bought for £10 and resigned to driving around the drives and fields for two lads aged 14 and 10.

This early experience provided for hours of fun. We stripped off the decayed bodywork and made a plywood fishtail back, lowered the steering rake and installed a small radiator to create a dragster style front end. Endless hours of restoring, and cleaning up mechanicals and electrics, provided for a hobby with some end result: learning how to drive. The three-speed 'crash' box for proper gear change, the acceleration factor helped by a skimmed cylinder head and a mighty Stromberg carburettor (5/-) on a special manifold, and then wet grass for controlled skid and drifting on 'ten tenths'… all laid a foundation for some serious motoring!

My first car for the road, an Austin 35, had to be purchased from my mother from a minuscule private income fund but at least meant that I was mobile. The graduation to the 100/6 Healey in Canada was a big step and of course driving on the right. The first adventure was taking the car down to the US for the midsummer months of 1960 and here I had my first experiences with the fuzz.

I was driving around at healthy speeds until caught out entering NYC from Long Island drifting round a flyover. The cops were more than interested in the car, me and my international driving licence covered in seals and crests, and it turned out that one had been stationed in Nottingham during the War. On the assurance that we all still wore 'Derrby hats' and that I wouldn't drive so recklessly again I was let go. With the exception of turning up 5th Avenue the wrong way with the Healey top down amongst the biggest American cars ever, and being advised very philosophically by a taxi driver 'if I werr you buddy, I'd turrn around,' I had an event-free summer until motoring back up to Canada.

For interest, I was on the old roads which wound through the woods and over the hills of New England… great contours and bends for getting the Healey really moving, often working with the excellent feature of overdrive on third and fourth gears in the four-speed box. Not much mirror work until I suddenly saw the sheriff hanging on for grim death. I threw up my hands in mock surrender and pulled over.

He'd obviously been enjoying himself, and after 'Now see here Charlie boy', further intrigue over the international licence and a short trip for him up the road, I was on my way fine free.

On my return to the UK, and after some juggling around, I managed to buy a second hand XK140 – BRG, black soft top and a C type engine. (Cars of this grade were relatively inexpensive as the maintenance and insurance costs were very heavy after the initial capital purchase – which is where the golden goose came in with mechanics at the mill garage and fleet rates for the latter.) This was a real road-going heavyweight with little to fault it except for the drum brakes. Rattling through the night, top down, straight-through exhausts throbbing away… wow!

Highlight journey: Goostrey to Berkeley Square 8.30 a.m./11.45 a.m. – 182 miles, with just the Coventry Bypass and the first bit of the M1 approaching London featuring as modern roads. Then it was dipped headlights on in the fast lane, flicking people out of one's way. Aston Martin tested their sports-racing cars from Newport Pagnell, and once left me well and truly trailing; they were travelling at over 160 mph!

I went back to a Healey which had now been bored out to 3 litres. A very sprightly ice-blue carriage until… CRASH! My first wedding eve and I got entangled with a small Triumph Herald with three lads up, hurtling in to Manchester. I'm in a line of traffic, they all flee, lads are okay and I'm unconscious in a local hospital.

The neurosurgeon – 'I'll see him in the morning' – got the sister in charge onto our fine Doctor who raced over and had me transferred immediately to the Manchester Royal Infirmary – thank you, sister. I came round for a bit and passed out for a further spell, particularly after a vicar peered over the screen… was the curtain going down?

Next, there was an operation to stitch up the head. 'Now we only work on locals for this, Nigel. As the head is connected to the heart, it's going to hurt like hell.' You can say that again, but the great diversion was a pretty probationer nurse standing on the team. Her eyes were out on stops, her face went paler by the second, and I thought she was going to be sick. I managed a smile and she slipped her hand under the sheet and held mine. The next painful bit was a nurse pulling out my silk shirt, thread by thread, from my chest and lower abdomen.

A few days later I was over the hump, when one might have run down and off the cliff, and back on the recovery curve. I had to lie very still and not move… but I'd risked a little recce, wished a very sick old boy well who actually died the next day, and had discovered the bathroom. A bed bath was looming, but I managed to wangle the proper variety through the consultant, 'provided you don't mind a nurse escorting you and watching over you'. 'Not at all,' says I, 'maybe I can select, and I don't think it's going to be you, Matron.' – who was accompanying him on his rounds. So there I am in this wonderful, steaming, old-fashioned tub and there she is sitting on a stool with the door ajar. 'I'm not sure I can manage the loofah, perhaps you'd like to bath me?' A charming blush… and the door closed.

Sad to report, this unfortunate episode is sometimes quoted as part of gossip, usually female. 'Steer clear of him, got banged on the nut you know.' Is this a bit of that old bug envy? Stick to your gardening, bridge table and pushing old 'Bertie' around in his wheelchair.

Now I was going to be in terrible pain, headaches for the rest of my life (never have – thank you, wonderful surgeon Mr Johnson) and should drive a simple car. But, the local station being at the bottom of the drive, I was able to key into Coventry via Crewe and buy a very clean XK150… well I was over 21! This was a serious upgrade on the 140, particularly with disc brakes, and provided for some fun motoring.

I graduated to a company car in the form of a 3.4 saloon Jaguar, and moved through the ranks of 3.8 and 4.2 E types. But the speed limits were now in and the days of driving properly on the roads were over. A highlight trip of this period: Haydock to Lockerbie, early June morning, 135 miles, 1 hr 30 mins, which meant cruising through the Cumbrian sweeps of the new M6 at anything up to 150 mph. The Lamborghini Espada belonged to a client, and was obviously his first sports car – he drove back!

Earlier I promised you the Mustang story: heading into Albany, NY, from the north, dry road, 8 p.m., very cold, getting late for date, cruising steadily along, no traffic, 100 + mph. Suddenly, blue light on back horizon, and in he zooms. Hysterical, 'get out of the car, you're under arrest, put your hands up, we're going to jail'… all this with gun in hand. We leave the Thruway and my car, and end up in a small bungalow at the side of a village in the woods. I'm sitting in a tiny study and in comes a wee man, announcing himself with 'Stand up, the court's now in session, how do you plead?' The sheriff was standing guard in the corner, and 'You're going to jail' kept on coming into the tirade from the 'bench'.

After a cooling-off period, and a lad summoned from the Fort Orange Club with my $100 fine, I ended up on the winterised porch, scotch in hand, having a very friendly conversation with the 'judge' (blue-collar foreman) and his wife.

Cars 'I have owned' then became practical à la pocket, including some powerful roadsters, a MkVI Bentley, no car when living in the Big Apple, and today a medium-sized 4x4 which is comfortable, and at the same time rugged for countryside things. If I went back to the old days equivalent I would probably lose my licence in ten minutes, and surely it's not what the car looks like, but what gets out of it which counts. Sloane Rangers in their Hummers (aka Slummers) take note!

One more highlight: this century, Nairn to Ross-on-Wye, 512 miles, 7 hrs including a fuel stop… you can do the sums for yourself and bear in mind the overall speed limit of 70 mph.

The racing urge was recently fulfilled with an afternoon at Oulton

Park. A souped-up saloon drive impressed the instructor: 'this is really very good for someone as young as Nigel Kenyon' (86%), followed by some serious (for me anyway) laps in a Formula single seater. 'I could really have got into this,' says I. 'Yes, you could, Nigel, and would have got to such a level that you would probably be dead by now… fried alive!'

So there I was heading for six years' bachelor life. Local daughters worked from home, younger divorcees needed comfort, and good old Crewe station provided the link with London for the weekenders. (I never reached the level of a friend who was seen seeing a girlfriend off on one platform, with the replacement moving in on the opposite side.) This included couples who could come to stay and make up small house parties, and also what we unkindly called the 'Fulham failures'. They bought flats and even houses with paltry alimony or legacy. How right they were. A marriage or so later, even now as elderly widows, 'I've always kept my flat,' the best investment they ever made! Talking of flats, nothing can be more generous than a life-long friend who would lend me his luxurious Knightsbridge variety. 'I'm going to be away, just help yourself.'

One friend brought her twin sister who declared, 'I'm not missing out on this,' and joined us after lights out. I astonished my great-aunt by leaving her grandson's wedding with a girl on each arm and being seen bundling them into a hardtop E type Jaguar, heading for home – legs flying in the air as the low sills contrived, all knickers and nonsense. The same vehicle was once the stage for very intimate moments across the front seats. Try it; Houdini would have been amazed! Three girls came to stay on a local promotion, pretty as anything, the leader outstanding and a daughter of a prominent politician. Sunday morning it was papers and breakfast all focused around their host's king-size cot.

A motor racing enthusiast – she and her equally attractive sister had both driven, sometimes as partners, in international racing events – had a fun flat in London which she shared with a prominent socialite gal. The latter was having an on/off walkout with an HisRH.

This was not the same HRH who used to keep trysts with a European actress at a character flat belonging to a dear friend. The latter who, in her bachelor-girl days prior to marrying into one of America's oldest families, could actually model stockings for Henri Bendel, had legs which were some of the finest ever on view. On average American female legs are world leaders.

I was staying and, after a most jolly dinner party, we were all tucked away in our respective double quarters for the night, only to be awakened by violent banging on the door. I was despatched to deal with the situation which required guiding His well-oiled Highness back to the lift advising him that his 'beloved' was at the other end of the flat, but would no doubt call him in the morning. She was in fact not alone, and the prominent industrialist friend of all told me next morning that he had heard the commotion and taken refuge in the wardrobe!

The last, a rackets player and excellent shot, catalysed a trip for the cads of the village to Spain by bringing the necessary in from abroad. (The economy was being run at the time by a bunch of amateurs and there was a limit of £10 – a major round of drinks – per capita to take away on holiday.) The concrete corridor was non-existent, the Marbella Club, Los Monteros and Attalya Park were new, Soto Grande had just finished the golf course and two adjoining houses, and I had a very jolly time with an Italian.

I visited her in Italy soon after, but on rather a formal basis. I was met by her in a coach-built sports Lancia and, having bought me an English newspaper with the car parked on the main street pavement in Padua, her door was ceremoniously opened by the traffic cop with his eyes firmly fixed on the 'sill'! All well so far, but I was then deposited in a small but very comfortable hotel penthouse suite, and a car was going to collect me for dinner chez her parents. This was all very fine, correct, unmarried Italian stuff. Speaking French with the younger ones, white gloved service for the dining room, visit to their extensive business, trips out to Venice and also to the suite, for which there was no bill, despite my rather feeble protestations. I followed up by joining her in Cortina in the spring, but retired hurt, literally off the slope. On return through London I hobbled into my cancer-dying grandmother's room and raised the last big laugh of her life. 'Just what the hell have you been up to now? Skiing in Italy, Kate. Really, what's her name?'

Two years later I revisited Guadalmina, this time my companion flying in from the US with her golf clubs. Two girls immediately greeted me from our previous visit, but it was mutual commiseration time for them as they were both going ex. Yes, we'd spotted it all previously, although one hubby must have ended up with a very tricky little number if she was the same who was hanging on to him like a limpet... BUT who had sought 'advice' from one of our party!

Summer 1970 I was introduced to Maryan. She was an Ozzie, living and working in London on a look-see mission. The top female end of things were finding it all a bit tame in Oz, what with frosties, cold ones, stubbies, snags et al.

Maryan was certainly a classic. She was an outstanding pianist, who had studied at master class level with Claudio Arrau, with all round musicianship to match. Her looks were an amalgamation of Sophia Loren and Raquel Welch, and she had just finished with Sadruddin Aga Khan, technically an uncle of the present Aga, after attending the latter's wedding in Paris. He had sent his private plane for the royal party which was headed up by HRH Princess Margaret – who did not like being upstaged by the girl from down under when the snappers ignored her on arrival! [b10] [b11]

We had a great engagement and decided to get married on 22 July 1971. Her parents came over several weeks prior and, as her Dad was an enthusiastic, very steady 6 handicap golfer, I was asked to arrange a trip round Scotland to include Turnberry, Gleneagles, St Andrews and some fillers in between.

Well, couldn't I just, and the zenith was arriving at Gleneagles in my MKVI Bentley with the manager waiting for us on the doorstep. 'Now maybe the ladies would like to just freshen up and then follow me'… into the prime window table for late lunch. My stock probably dropped a bit when I beat my future father-in-law at St Andrews. He had arranged this through his membership of the Royal Melbourne, and I returned a gross 78 which was a record for me.

The Bentley featured again in Bond Street when parked on the double line outside my intended's favourite boutique – Yves Saint Laurent. The traffic warden was just sharpening his pencil, when two lackeys laden with parcels swung out of the shop with the delighted purchaser in pursuit. Notebook away, he opened the door for her whilst I helped load up the boot and the back seat!

We had a short breather and then off to Oz, starting with New York. This featured a variety of friends entertaining us, culminating with a big buffet supper reception. Next Salt Creek Ranch in Texas, followed by Mexico City and a short tour into the countryside. We were mobbed at the bullfight and pelota evenings, not on my account – although catcalls and whistles are very good for morale. Six nights on a near as dammit private island off Fiji, where the owner was also staying at the time, and Melbourne here we are.

Keeping it simple, this lasted a bare six months. Great receptions all round, trips up to Sydney, Christmas on the beach. BUT two real minuses: (a) nobody wanted to employ me and (b) I discovered that my 'bride' did not like the technical aspect of being actually married. There were two clues. I discovered that whilst we were still in England she had visited a counsellor about post-wedding blues (sort of postnatal), and I just happened to see her getting out of a black Porsche sports car in the drive of the Sydney flat, after lunch, and she wasn't the driver. I returned to GB and we were divorced, by post, in October 1974.

(She never remarried... but started into the pop/country music business and was encouraged by, er, 'Ol blue eyes' to move to California. This she did, ran her own band for some time and ended up living in Woodbridge Canyon, Beverly Hills... view down to Hollywood, cliff-side swimming pool, vast private recording studio. A number of years later I visited her and boyfriend when on West Coast trips from NYC, the latter sending me a very sweet email when she subsequently died of cancer in 1998.)

I returned to GB via Singapore, stopping for four nights of 'rest and repair' in old Raffles Hotel, and a charming American woman just happened to be passing through. They had a wonderful restaurant and, as she was also going ex, we were able to have several commiserative dinners.

Who was there to meet me at Heathrow?... an old friend who had been one of my ushers, and a rackets player – 'What ho sporty, the spare room's all yours.' I was only just ahead of a mutual friend of ours who arrived back from New York after a marriage that had lasted, er, only a few weeks. He was relegated to the sofa.

However, he soon picked himself up, moved in with a gal who sported an Italian butler and a drop-head Bentley, and during the next twenty-five years became extremely successful... cobbling together a plc, leading in his own Grand National winner, and arriving in Seaport NYC with his own 135 ft five-deck motor yacht to entertain 'the troops' from John Street. Sadly Rocky died having not quite reached 60... over-cooking the pudding or one late night too many – sportsmen beware! At least Tim and self are still alive.

After trying London through the generosity of friends, it was back to Cheshire and I just happened to get into, and ultimately purchase, a lodge belonging to friends 'up at the big house'. Use of the tennis court, ideally placed in the country for a short commute to my offices, watch all the horse activity without having to be involved (except for occasional round-ups when they all escaped), and called the 'lodger' by my friend and landlord Peter, particularly when having a cocktail with his wife, Gillian, on his return from the office. A delightful family with whom I integrated, and even helped baby sit for late teenagers on occasions, but, of course, on my best behaviour. The pretty eldest, Julie, was always bubbling with energy, and has since written several books. [b12] Social life took off and one was in the centre of sporting activity as will be revealed in later chapters.

Significant heiresses, sleek older divorcees (two in particular who passed the three tests... and some), a lady explorer, old and new friends from the US, a Cabinet Minister's daughter, a lady MI5 agent, a soprano opera singer and representation from Europe were part of the scene.

The last always had a different curiosity and friendliness, sometimes leading to farce where fortunately senses of humour held intact... like shaving in a substantial Belgian Schloss bathroom when in walks my hostess's husband – they were supposedly living apart, but he'd just popped in to collect some clothes. A birthday dinner for a Dutch friend (she was also a useful squash player) and along comes a very attractive German, who had in fact introduced us as a substitute for an earlier relationship. Dinner was grand, hilarious and the whole evening ended very much à trois!

Another German relationship was not only very charming, but also gave me an interesting insight into how the upmarket German had survived the Second World War. Some did and some just didn't, but right through families stuck together and supported each other. This was particularly the case with my companion's mother. They had left a substantial property with big acreage and Schloss to match marooned back behind what became the Iron Curtain, fleeing on a tractor towing two trailers with some basics and the children, my friend a baby in an egg basket. Mother moved into a small bungalow on the edge of the village belonging to the more fortunate cousins – household name financiers, the Bethmanns based in Frankfurt – and daughter Yelka subsequently, after a divorce of her own, had a flat in the stables to help as secretary to the estate.

We were always included in events at Schonstadt which was run on a big scale. The Baronin played the cello exceptionally well, and two students used to come in from Marburg University to make up the quartet with her and an elderly musician who came for the summer, and also acted as tutor and companion for the children. He also took 'plays', and these were performed for the family and friends using the upstairs drawing rooms as the stage by incorporating the dividing doors. The children acting completely uninhibited (one memorable Sherlock Holmes in German) was really wonderful, accompanied by the bearded Baron chuckling away – 'ah das ist sehr komisch!'

We were also on the hospitality circuit which included a big society ball (white tie or 'uniform') in a vast establishment – only snag the dances were mainly quadrilles and polkas. Sylvester (New Year) with the Wittgensteins at their country home. We arrived early and three liveried characters were lighting candles on high trees in the hall. In the courtyard at the back, lit by rather eerie side lights, lay fifteen wild boar – the bag for the New Year shoot. I was invited for this the following year but sadly had to decline.

Amongst all this fun I had to adopt a paternal role, not on one but two fronts – not what you're thinking! One of those 'can you see me in London' calls confirmed that my first ex was divorcing her second husband, and hopefully I would take a much closer role with our Philip. She had bred four more children and had her hands well and truly full.

Well, of course I could – yes, and even come to the divorce hearing and give a reference to help her case along with regard to his custody – what a sport! Thereafter he would come to me for part of his school holidays.

(Elizabeth married for a third time and died in 2000. She struggled with cancer for some twelve years, battling with three doses of chemotherapy over the period… must be a record. Philip was the only speaker at her funeral. He had his text bound, and merely reading it years after can get the old chin wobbling a bit. How he delivered it, and then marched down the aisle in front of 200+ people to accompany a beautiful Handel soprano aria on the organ, may become apparent when we get to the performing aspects of our lives later on. Not a flicker of emotion other than a light smile to guests – some nerve!)

The other concerned my first cousin Charlie Kenyon. His father had died when he was only 16 and this had set off a series of depressions. He had to leave school, found it very difficult to get a job, and had to spend some time in a sanatorium where I used to visit him – I even suggested that he might like to live with me out in the country, away from the pressures and temptations of London. His financial position was such that he was not just making a little go 'a long way', but 'practically nothing go ten bloody miles'… not easy, believe me!

However he soldiered on, and got engaged to a sweet girl who had plenty of background to support his nice nature. With no father and his first uncle unable to attend (my father, who was coping with my mother beginning to fail with cancer), I stepped in and off to jolly old Suffolk. A few little pep talks (from me!), lots of gas and laughs with his young friends, and the day went well. A niece of one of his godmothers (another, Rosalind Russell the actress, was by then deceased) was over from Canada, and happened to be staying in my hotel. Well, ten days later I was representing the family again, this time at his funeral. He had gone out from his honeymoon hotel to watch the RAC motor rally and been steamrollered by a truck in a narrow country lane. Sarah remarried later and the curtain came down on a very sad little episode.

A trip to the US in 1984 had reignited my fascination with the country coupled, of course, by a chance meeting… and so, early 1985, I moved over to NYC, which features later in the all American chapter.

6 Sporting Profile

'But canstow playen racket to and fro?' (Chaucer)

As you will have already gathered, games and sporting activities have played a big part in my life. Underlying natural talent has probably not been exploited to the full, but the ability to take a hand, join in, or make up the four has always given pleasure.

After school I was fortunate to be able to continue with my racquet games, particularly rackets.

This is an obscure game, so often confused by the uninitiated with racquetball, paddle tennis and other such banal pastimes. Rackets is dangerous, difficult and expensive. It is played in a large (30 ft x 60 ft) dark, indoor court – similar markings and play to squash – with a white hard ball that can be struck at speeds up to 160 mph. It's dangerous and difficult because of the potentially lethal speed and hardness of the ball, and expensive because a missed hit can easily shatter the delicate wooden-framed racquet. The scarceness of courts – Canada 1, US 8, UK 28 – makes it a rarefied game, as all of Canada, the US and only three in the UK (The Queen's Club [b13], Manchester Tennis & Racquet Club and Seacourt Tennis Club) are private clubs. The balance in the UK are situated at top boys' boarding schools. (Please don't think of that chippy word 'privileged'... try 'lucky'.)

I was lucky to be based, from both home and office standpoint, close to Manchester.

This enabled me to join in serious club play with older players, and team up with one of the all-time amateur greats, Peter Kershaw. He had won numerous amateur singles and doubles events, the latter often with his then world-champion partner David Milford.

We used to play against the schools on a hectic but fun weekend schedule: Rugby – his and David's old school – on the Saturday, beat the first pair, have a bottle of beer – Peter owned a brewery – and then beat the second pair. Continue to Malvern for Sunday and go through the same routine. The latter had by then taken on Ronnie Hughes as the professional, who had come from Manchester and continued by successfully coaching winning pairs for many years. He also had coached me as a schoolboy, is still alive (85), and always his wonderful self. He witnessed another entry for their match book, this time some forty years on, when I was entered again as a winner over the first pair. The Kershaw/Kenyon combination never lost a match.

Rackets was also included in visits to the US and the 'weekends' were especially good fun. The Tuxedo Park weekend in February was, and still is, one of the favourites. This wooded and walled enclave, of c.1500 acres, was established as a commutable country estate from NYC for the mega $ocial stars. Naturally the tennis club included both a rackets and a real tennis court, alongside the fine parkland golf course. Lakes were hockey rinks and general skating in the winter, whilst the guard at the gate always announces guests, even from several miles' range!

1967 was a vintage year. I managed to lose the final of the 'Rackets Spittoon', much to the annoyance of my peppery older partner Clary Pell – I was still the young 'un. I met an adventurous gal who just provided so much fun and laughter, and also met my great friend Edward Ulmann. He had just been married and strolled into the dedans of the real tennis court with his wife, Priscilla, and mother-in-law both appropriately clothed in long fur coats. Outside the hand-some roaring fireplace ambience of the clubrooms, Tuxedo racquets galleries and the dedans are cold places.

The dancing and parties are well organised, and the ladies always seem to be full of 'mountain air'. I often think of a prominent socialite jumping onto a piano, talk about knickers and nonsense... good old Tuxedo Park! I won the spittoon doubles in 1980, and this meant a first-time rackets tourney win for a late US newcomer to the game, Randolph 'you can never be too slow on the backswing' Jones. He's still a scratch golfer and always cheery.

Boston Tennis & Racquets weekend was another attractive venue. The best stay was in a large town house, all fully operational... but I had been warned. Our elderly host was very concerned about fire, so any guests were always taken round personally to inspect the fire escapes. He demonstrated the opening of various windows and then threw out a rope ladder. Each guest had to follow suit, even the girls, who were giggling so much – great lessons in self-control. Breakfast time the butler was always on hand particularly with a bowl of ice cubes for the Sealyham, who crunched these under his master's feet with great delight, to be subsequently fed with large slices of bacon from his plate!

I have always been made most welcome in Chicago. The final of the US amateur doubles in 1981 was a big highlight (at least for me) in front of the packed Sunday afternoon gallery of enthusiasts, topped off by the Winnetka and Lake Forest 'leaders'.

The match was set up on the then current world champion John Prenn (still a ranked player today) and Tom Pugh v. Willie Surtees (ex-world champion) and yours truly. We lost 1-3, but no games below 10 and several to the set. My old friend George Hendrick, who moved into the Club at the time of divorce in the late 1970s, still lives there!

Lots more rackets followed, including play back in the US as described in later chapters... and even now. Two highlights in the oldies stage: 15/10 winners in the last, best of 7 at Eton two years ago, and 'you've got one of the best eyes ever, Nigel, bet not many high pheasants get past you' – coming off court in the 2006 over-sixties doubles. Well, thank you... rather doubtful, but nice idea anyway and certainly very good for morale!

Exposure to rackets led me to real tennis (US 'court' tennis). This is the Henry VIII Hampton Court variety, depicted as 'Tennis balls, my liege' (Shakespeare) and 'My mistress is a tennis ball composed of cotton fine' (Shadwell). There are courts in: Australia 6, France 3, UK 26, US 9. If you want to know the fundamentals, go and see for yourself. To learn how to score, you'd better get on court and play!

Several courts, including Queen's, Manchester and Seacourt, are adjacent to rackets courts, so tournament weekends can have both running simultaneously. The game can be properly handicapped and one can go on playing for ever. Deaths on court do happen and octogenarian doubles feature at several venues. The US locations are all private clubs and similarly in the UK (more or less) there are several gems, one of the more outstanding being Moreton Morrell in Warwickshire. This is set in the country at the bottom of the drive of a substantial mansion, and was built by an American, Charles Garland, in 1905 as a further gesture to becoming an instant English country gent. My own play is way down the list, but very enjoyable. [r4]

Lawn tennis – which includes clay, hard courts, or mats – was never encouraged in schools and was only prompted from home and then in later life, either around clubs or private courts. In Cheshire we had any number of the latter backed by senior clubs in the Manchester suburbs. This provided for above average social tennis on a regular basis throughout the summer… sometimes even on grass. A friend had a pair of grass courts which was ideal for asking eight, and hence same sex doubles or mixed.

I have recently met up again with Alastair after thirty-five years, via a picture in a shooting magazine of him looking out at the world over the top of a dead antelope! 'There are lots of deaf old colonels here in Wiltshire, and I'm one of them'… only two years older than me! No more rackets or tennis for him, but shooting in the UK and South Africa, and following bullfighting in Spain. It certainly takes all sorts, and all the more fun when we can still have a very good laugh. He was divorced some fifteen years ago, and prefers his girlfriends to be 'stick-thin'. I personally prefer the 'fuller figure'. There is something rather appealing about the erstwhile super-model shape that has, er, filled out a bit. Lucky our respective mothers, who were in daily contact on the telephone, are not around to hear these g&t-lubricated stories of the old, and even not so old, days.

A socially acceptable team from Cheshire once travelled to Jersey for a week's fun, and chartered a plane for a trip to Dinard. We played against the club, which included some French ex-Davis Cup players, and were treated to a semi-formal lunch with the Mayor. Luckily we did not have to play afterwards or indeed drive the plane! Our other games were on private courts and I stayed one evening to have dinner with our hostess… she came to Cheshire for a return match soon after. Jersey was always fun to visit; various deceased old tycoons had left much younger widows.

Playing overseas is always in a climate which, although warmer, seems to spur one on. Looking at the pyramids over the fence in Egypt, various Spanish venues, Australia, the US, and a memorable afternoon in Chicago, 95 degrees Fahrenheit and humidity to match. My pretty partner, Jane, sister of a dear friend, Anne, had obviously played big time. 'My last competitive game was going out to Rosie

Casals in the third round!' Our opponents were to match her… so all stops out Kenyon, who was just able to survive the serious 'buzzing' building up in the back of my skull.

Golf should be enjoyed and not endured, and at the same time needs a regular two games a week to maintain an improving standard. Quite simply I have just played fine weather golf and never enough to go lower than the 15 handicap, break 90 but never 80, mark. Nevertheless this has provided pleasure and enough enthusiasm to 'take the clubs'. Spain, Australia, the US have featured. A big drawback with the last on the upper East Coast: courses close for the winter and open again in April if you're lucky, not much bang for hefty bucks. I say hefty as often the course can be an integral part of a country club scene, but again this may still only be a summertime facility.

In Zimbabwe I have enjoyed Leopard's Rock, where you look down the hills into the sinister wilderness of Mozambique. Also Royal Harare, a fine parkland course close to the city, and the adjacent country course Chapman's. The last has the extra hazards of crocodiles sunning themselves alongside various water hazards… no scooping out that wayward shot here.

A recent find is golf in Normandy in spring. Go inland a bit, other than the usual around Deauville, and take in some pretty woodland courses with azaleas to match… pretend you're at Augusta.

Sadly the development of B-grade courses in GB, trying to provide farmers with a diversification and support second-rate country hotels, is just one worse than Spain where courses are being crammed into little valleys with concrete veeyas as scenery. At least the sun shines and there are the fine original courses.

Balance and timing got me into skiing, which started well and provided for some holidays in France, Switzerland, Italy and Norway, several repeats, and one-offs in the US. But there was always that nagging apprehension of doing some damage and putting the rest of the summer, even the rest of one's lifetime sporting activities, at risk. Other dangers were emerging in the form of overcrowded slopes, fuelled by drunkenness and yobbish behaviour. An American friend was crippled for life… and he was standing still!

However, I am going to resurrect this, incorporated in all-round winter excursions.

The focus will be on trail skiing, on ice skating by trying to upgrade the current forwards and backwards only routine, hopefully fulfilling a lifetime ambition of travelling in bobsleighs, and even driving oneself solo on the skeleton!

7 Play – The Countryside

'The huntsman winds his horn, and a-hunting we will go' (Fielding)

Fox-hunting

What was a regular pastime of my paternal grandfather's generation skipped my father and his brothers and consequently never really got me going. My first recollection of horses was at the end of the Second World War when eight hunters belonging to my great-uncle Geoff arrived to stay, managed by his head groom Herbert. Why they came I never knew, but I can certainly still remember Uncle Geoff. He was jovial, exuded kindness and I am sure that this quality must have been sensed by his horses. He was not in touch with the Mill, other than clipping coupons (dividends) and such reported classics as 'oh bugger the looms, let's go and get some lunch' when a family meeting was overrunning. He just loved horses and taking them fox-hunting. Apart from his fine stables near Malton, he kept a few in livery near Market Harborough in Leicestershire and Tarporley in Cheshire for the away invitations. He never disposed of them, and when he died there were forty still in his care, active or retired. Some had been successful in the show arena, such as a 'Hunter of the Year' travelling with four other stable-mates to the old Madison Square Garden – long before air transport.

Herbert was my first outside 'god'. I watched him in the stables with these magnificent animals and riding them out often on a double leading rein. He was very keen to get me started with a children's pony, but this was not to be, and suddenly the whole team had gone back to Yorkshire. My personal riding experience did extend to some childhood riding, and recently a day on a polo pony under professional supervision to see if I could hit the ball. I could... and could not walk for the following week!

So, although hunting featured very much in the social structure of home and surrounding life, I was never an actual participant, albeit so close as to learn and understand the mechanics in great detail, alongside other country exposure.

It was very easy, however, to recognise the type, and there was (and, er, still is) talk such as 'I've been hunting for forty years' (so bloody what?), 'Vermin control, don't yah know' (it isn't) and 'Us' (yes, us... who the hell is that?). I have always felt that this rather cavalier attitude was not helping the social changes which were being directed in a stance against hunting in principle – or even just the type who was taking part.

Either way it was banned as from 2005, merely allowing drag hunting – aka 'chasing old socks'. This pantomime is sometimes watched by an eagle owl, sitting on a quad bike and looking very confused, in order to qualify some ridiculous technicality. I am not even going to elaborate on the disgraceful promotion of shooting foxes with shotguns. Could this all have been averted? Answer possibly yes, but would have needed flexibility to accommodate modern times and also, a most important factor, climate change.

A scene such as: No more bagging (hey, we never do that... oh yes you do, I've watched it happening), no more digging out (particularly after going to earth), no more cub-hunting (it's not cubbing), and as for 'autumn hunting', change the season to the end of February (warmer spring ergo earlier litters), and one might have been able to hunt November/February. Let's hope that this current farce can be redirected on these lines.

Shooting

Although there was no organised shooting at home, or indeed an estate structure, the house was surrounded by farming and situated in the middle of the Cheshire countryside.

This scenario required outside maintenance for hedges, ditches, and other jobs separate from the garden. Step up my other outside 'god' and mentor, Mr Holdsworth.

This fine man had been head keeper for a serious shoot in Lancashire, which had been disbanded on the death of the owner. Here was a fountain of knowledge that far outweighed schoolrooms, and I waited for him eagerly at 9 a.m. prompt during my early school holidays. The curriculum was varied: watching and discussing scything techniques, also sharpening of same... running ferrets with all the details such as muzzling, lining, use of nets... gutting and skinning hares and rabbits... bird and animal recognition, such as parting the grass on a bank and revealing a hen pheasant sitting on her nest, magic... slaying of poultry and geese with major involvement of his assistant catching up the latter, and watching whilst they were bled over a bucket. Instant death with the red knife from his waistcoat pocket was sensitively explained. The knife was part of his saw that you needed 'your knife, a piece of string and half a crown (2/6d) in your pocket, and you're fit for the hunting field' – on his retirement he presented me with the knife!

Shooting started for real as rough shooting, with our old spaniel and my mother's 20 bore. [b14] This was a lightweight gun, beautifully balanced, with a similar range to a 12. My first lesson in safety came when I saw my father disappearing into the potatoes clutching his neck. I had killed a rabbit in the cow lane at the side of the field which he was beating towards me, with the pattern simultaneously hitting a puddle and a pellet ricocheting at right angles a further forty yards. Luckily he was still in a starched collar, although the pellet had penetrated this to the second layer… so no damage done.

My first pheasant day was as a substitute. I had been asked by our friend the Doctor to go beating, but bring my gun along for pigeons in the evening. On arrival a gun had not turned up. I was asked to join in, hit my share and had a memorable evening in the pigeon wood. And so it went on, averaging about twenty formal days per winter, with the exception of less when overseas, although several fine days were had in Belgium.

The shoot belonged to a family with an extensive engineering business, primarily making looms. I was an obvious target as the director responsible for same, but the shooting aspect quickly developed away from pure commerce. I, and sometimes a lady companion, would be met in Brussels by a chauffeur-driven Mercedes which was at my disposal for the whole weekend. The guesthouse was more than comfortable and the shooting excellent. King (then Prince) Albert used to attend with Paola, and one year the TV was discreetly making a documentary… featuring in a small part le jeune anglais! Pheasant bags were anything from 500–1000 pheasants, sometimes with partridges thrown in. I once went for a hare driving day and over 100 were shot. Not so many you may say, but these were driven out of roots over flat meadows towards the guns, and the stock had been speeded up by importation of breeding jacks from Poland. These monsters weighed up to ten pounds and ran like cheetahs and so did their offspring. One day a Frenchman asked me to join his shoot the following day… on a Sunday!

There we were in a small classic village just over the border over-looking Lille, 9 a.m., all getting assembled from our transport amidst dogs and the usual, with the padre pulling the bell outside a small church across the square. The nature of the steep valleys allowed for driving the birds uphill, releasing at the top and hurtling down over the guns either side and over the top of the wood. After each drive, my host would march downhill chatting to his guests and surreptitiously counting the bag for that drive. I am pleased to say that I shot my share of the day's bag of 563.

Shooting in the US was also fun. [b15] The only driven pheasant shoot of any consequence is out on Long Island near Southampton – The Port of Missing Men. Boundaries of the sea and marsh lakes on two sides make for easier vermin control and, provided there is some wind, the ground is laid out and maintained for some good covert shooting, which yields bags of c.250. The marsh aspects also provide some excellent duck shooting, mainly wild as this tip of the island is a natural stopping off and holding place for migratory birds, as well as ideal for quickly accepting released birds into a wild habitat. A mixture of Racquet Club cronies and other experienced US shots (there are some… and they can be very experienced) made up the teams.

My old friend Edward, however, took a bit of a hiding on a certain duck outing, when I was his guest for 250 on a wild and windy day. At half time I was in good form and wandered into the glade for the break. Birds were being laid out, and I asked a new friend how he was getting on: 'well, I've only got two so far,' was the reply. I'd opened with three right and lefts and carried on from there, as had my host. Reports from the eight stand minders seemed to indicate that only two or three of us were making meaningful contributions. The total pickup was 436!

One summer, on the same shoot, we shot pigeons in June. This involved surrounding a large wood, and then moving round to different pegs. The pigeons, which had been imported off the streets of NYC in a large hamper, were hurled into the air one after another. They shot up to an alarming height, circled the wood to get their bearings, and headed off back in the direction of the City… *c.*300 did not make it. Sort of live clays, and one day of this is enough. My lady companion over from Scotland was amazed, particularly at the cold lobster and white wine lunch on the beach afterwards!

Shooting in the UK has always been with friends, sometimes on shared days and paying syndicates for the season, depending on the state of the exchequer. As a private guest several hosts have been very generous. The spread has always provided for interest, as per the following notes condensed from my game book.

Anglesey, with 4 guns walking up to 4 standing guns, assisted by a motley group of beaters sloshing through reedy valleys. Result: snipe, a few pheasant, a hare or two, rabbits, teal, mallard. Imagine great wild duck flighting on the cliffs, with the rolling Atlantic beneath.

North Lancashire walking up wild English partridges through roots and disused coal mines… they like these for the warmth and gritty feeding.

Cheshire for some good covert shoots at rather grand houses. Even a little grouse moor only 12 miles from the centre of Manchester. Shropshire always showed coverts of quality and more rolling terrain.

North Wales for fine covert shooting, like going right to the top for grouse, pheasants (best cocks only days of 250+ on both Friday and Saturday – six guns, one gun each, driving snow, howling wind) and lots of laughs.

Smallest official day… 16 grouse, borrowed pointer, 1 beater (a very pretty girl), chicken and champagne lunch, 1 gun!

Other shooting will feature in subsequent chapters.

Do the ladies like shooting? Of course they do and several are becoming very good shots. They also like supporting, and this encourages you to shoot well. 'Good shot, darling,' is not only very good for morale, but the second half of the phrase more than encouraging if the relationship is just beginning to blossom.

Gamekeepers do have a fascination… a great friend's wife eloped with one. I met up with them again in Scotland where he ran an excellent shoot, this time as the host. His keeper actually shook my hand after one drive which brought birds off the side of a moor at stratospheric height. We (in the plural… but!) had shot 90 on a 150 bird day, and it was the first drive. I happened to draw the same spot the following year… and I did not hold back. [b16]

Try another one (not me), like coming back home a day early and finding your keeper rather adopting the role of master of your house… and actually wearing one of your suits!

But where's it all going? Yes, the general political/social aspect is gnawing away again, as are the antis. Are the shooting fraternity facing up to this or going the way of the fox-hunting folk? Can they self-regulate the messy level of some shooting back up to an irreproachable standard? I personally doubt it. Having followed the action for many years, I have been plugging the following which I feel should be presented to the authorities for official redirection, merely as a backdrop if required. A few in number, but sadly often greater in stature, are spoiling it for everybody.

1. Change shooting seasons, particularly pheasants Nov./Jan., grouse Sept./Nov., partridges Oct./Dec. Woodcock, snipe and hares only where enough and in a short season.
2. Release densities of birds to be properly controlled relative to the terrain in question. One cannot generalise on a set number per acre.

3. No topping up whatsoever during the seasons. Feed on after pheas ant season till May.

4. No tame ducks… i.e. shooting tame ducks off their own pool. Feed away into the wild and no flighting ponds already shot over.

5. No more caged rearing, bitting or specking, full stop.

6. Ban all forms of snares, use only official live or fenn traps. The notion that this would lead to poisoning and other unpleasant-ness is very lame. Some grown-up estates have already done so.

7. No pheasant shooting after 3 p.m. (the light turns, they all go to roost, what a surprise). So, encourage shooting through to lunch, and prevent prior alcohol excesses.

8. All under-16s to be properly monitored by an adult at all times until passing official proficiency certificates from qualified instructors… this to include fieldcraft.

9. Countryside Wardens, as per France, just to look in as required. If you're running things correctly… what's the worry?

10. Discourage shooting pheasants with two guns. This is entirely unnecessary as many game books would show and to which senior marksmen have admitted. The principle also applies to many partridge and grouse days. A companion merely 'stuffing' one gun can be quicker anyway. ([b17] A great read, but only history in modern times.)

If only the various countryside and shooting organisations could amalgamate or at least work together. Trustees and directors must get their heads out of the sand, or heather if in Scotland! Not wanting to be thought a sxxt by your chums by not taking a firm stand on some rigid redirection is a very weak way of letting everybody else down. Waving around pamphlets which 'we've all put together' talking about 'good practice' and 'assurance' will not solve the problem.

'I say, Nigel's gone all pinko'… er, sorry chaps, times have changed. Who has researched this subject behind the scenes for years, based on practical lifetime hands-on experience, both on the sharp end and out in the field? This includes interviews with the League Against Cruel Sports, the Middle Way, and also backing a police meeting to discuss violence against shooting and the Countryside generally.

Shooting joke: A cocky young blood, called Peregrine, is a guest in a very senior house party for a weekend's shooting. By dinnertime, even on the Friday night, other guests are so brassed off that they go through to the chef and replace his portion of the caviar first course with the pellets from a 12 bore cartridge. This is duly served and with a single flourish, accompanied by 'just like they do in Russia,' Peregrine downs his helping in one, toast and all.

Next morning at the elaborate breakfast proceedings, there is an empty seat at the table, and this continues through the porridge, bacon and eggs stages. Guests are just starting the toast and second cup of coffee when in staggers Peregrine, pale and rather dishevelled. 'Ah, there you are, Peregrine,' beams the hostess, 'we've been expecting you. Did you have a poor night?' 'Well, er, no thank you,' says Peregrine, 'but I'm sorry to report that coming downstairs just now, I broke wind and have shot your cat.'

Fishing

First came on to the menu in the late 1980s and started in New York. A crash day course with Orvis (obviously buying their equipment afterwards) and away we went. This started immediately in upstate NY near Millbrook – sort of Sussex and Wiltshire all rolled into one. Imagine a river with plenty of character and incorporated in an old-established family estate. The river flows through meadows, then down gorges in the woods, and into a holding pond with a fine complementary hut in the middle. Next a waterfall and then 3 miles run through to Millbrook itself. Trout were plentiful, challenging to catch, but all made for an easily accessible day out from the City.

A contrast to Tamarak Reserve was fishing on the Hudson river in the City itself. This was spasmodically with Cuban immigrants who had a wide variety of tackle and crab traps! The heavy-duty Abercrombie & Fitch spinning rod looked slightly out of place, until it caught. I had passed and we were on chuckling good terms, particularly when I gave them my catch. Two passers-by on the fine refurbished river walkway, Robert and Debbie Geline, were astonished at the 'social mix', and we have been friends ever since.

Salmon next and I decided to sponsor a trip to Scotland, taking a house party to the Isle of Lewis in the Outer Hebrides. This was composed of Brits and American friends and none had fished for salmon before. All were successful and several of the men also enjoyed the 'dogging' for grouse. I have continued fishing spasmodically as will be revealed later, enjoy it, but it is not a must do to go through hardy annual trips to the same place. Potential variety is one of the sport's big pluses. [r5]

For another contrast try for Tiger fish on the Zambezi, and your flat-bottomed aluminium boat gets grounded by a sand spit fifty yards from a group of five hippos, ankle deep, grazing off the bank. 'What do we do now?' – 'Get out and push, quick.' The two of us certainly did! The Zambezi is shallow, and that wave that can suddenly appear sweeping towards you means that a hippo has used its ability to sink itself, and is running along the bottom with evil intent. Again time for exit on full throttle!

Racing

In early days we attended point-to-points, local northern racecourses such as Chester and Aintree for the Grand National. Several friends rode as gentlemen amateurs in National Hunt ('under rules') and various lady friends also rode in the point-to-points. The real buzz however comes when one is connected, albeit in my case looking over the owners' shoulders.

The first exposure was to jump racing, which lasts longer... a five minute thrill rather than three as on the flat. It's 'for kicks rather than cups' (as I once suggested to our elegant lady trainer Venetia Williams – always the winner of the 'best turnout' and I mean her rather than the horse. She is very successful with the latter), and if you can't withstand a psychological battering of 90% disappointment, don't get involved... best watched.

This particular stable of horses has now moved to training with another delightful Herefordshire family business – the Scudamores. They all live together in various wings of a large house, surrounded by horses and fun. Grandfather Michael and father Peter were both Champion Jockeys in their own right, and a grandson, Tom, has already proved himself, hopefully to go on to even bigger things.

My flat racing experience has been greatly enhanced through my friend Jane, who is a member of the Royal Ascot Racing Club. They can own up to 6 horses, bought in as yearlings, managed by the Highclere Castle Stud, and then run until the end of their career or are sold off as 'horses in training'. ('One white foot – buy it, two white feet – try it, three white feet – think about it, four white feet – go home without it.') The Club have sole access to their own magnificent rooms at Ascot racecourse which are available, all found, for all the fixtures... including the Royal Ascot meeting in June. When their horses are racing elsewhere, facilities and badges are laid on accordingly.

I have recently attended the opening of the 'new' Ascot racecourse, which must qualify for one of the finest sporting venues in the world. Well done private enterprise. It was all built, including re-laying the track, in exactly two years. However, commercial greed seems to have downgraded the Royal Enclosure aspect significantly to swell the numbers with hoi polloi. Also, sad to report, the traditional 'racegoer' has got big ideas with stretch limos, boobbly and dressing up, or almost off as far as the girls go. The latter were responsible for starting brawling in the car park picnic areas, reminiscent of football hooligans… if only they would learn!

Now in 2005 when I became a 'connection' (aka in my case a 'hanger on') the RARC happened to own a good 'un – Motivator. He won the Derby… simple as that… and latterly was sold off for stud (now standing at the Royal Stud at Sandringham) for £6 million. This euphoric season also took us to Leopardstown in Ireland and Paris for the Arc. It was interesting to note that the other two in the string for that season were on the 'horses in training' tack, and were sold off for 1,500 gns and 2,000 gns. They originally cost 50,000 and 75,000 respectively… but that, as they say, is racing!

At Tattersalls of Newmarket all sale prices are still quoted in guineas, i.e. £1-1-0 in old GB money. A successful 40-year-old stockbroker recently owned up to not knowing what guineas were. Must be dinosaur talk!

8 Music – Classical

'Music, the greatest good that mortals know, and all of heaven we have below'

(Fielding)

Well, it has to be in to be in the blood, system, genes or whatever; and the following should prove this theory.

As hinted at earlier, great-grandmother was an excellent amateur pianist. She had trained at the conservatoire in Berlin and was on friendly terms with well-known European musical families such as Schumann and Wagner. She never played professionally, but spent many hours playing to herself and for other's enjoyment, as well as encouraging younger people at home and in the neighbourhood. My grandfather was the conduit for this artistic talent and he had a fine voice, which was channelled onto the stage.

My father was also a fine amateur pianist, and what one might term as a 'proper musician'. He could sight read at the very highest standard, and would regularly disappear to his music room after dinner and wind up the Bechstein, often for several hours. Great to listen to, but one felt that this was a form of escapism as he kept the subject very much to himself. He could also sing well, but never once did he offer to sing together or assemble a group for amateur social enjoyment. He had studied music at Cambridge as an additional course under Charles Wood.

Wood was a prolific composer, particularly of church music. Never a week goes by without some of his compositions featuring in the cathedral music lists down through to the ranks of parish churches. For instance, 'Hail Gladdening Light', 'Beati Quorum', 'O thou the Central Orb', 'This Joyful Eastertide'... even good old 'Ding Dong Merrily on High' – harmonized by Charles Wood.

He died of cancer in 1926 aged 57, prior to which a quartet of men from King's College Choir used to sing round his bedside. Dad was one of the last people to see him alive. 'When I entered his room it was obvious that he was very ill. We talked for a few minutes about Cambridge and local affairs, and I saw that he was tired and in discomfort. Before leaving him I held his hand, which was cold and thin, for a moment. "Thank you for coming, my dear boy", he said, and I left his room with tears in my eyes, and humility in my heart, knowing that I was leaving a great man for the last time.' Dad and a fellow undergraduate friend, also a pupil of Wood, helped Mrs Wood clear up his things. [b18]

Now the next generation did not play the piano other than prep school 'music lessons', but has always enjoyed singing. There is a singing CV in note form, purely assembled for the record... it is not a substitute for an audition. Conversely, I have turned up as a complete stranger to two distinctive parish churches, Kenilworth and Mere, and wound up singing evensong with their very adequate choirs... anthems, the lot!

(Charles *Nigel* Kenyon (b. 1941) started singing aged 9, treble private school choir. Years 13/18 alto and bass at Charterhouse – Dr John Wilson – main choir, choral soc., small choir (18 members). The last, half boys/half adults, included Bill Llewellyn, who concurrently ran the Linden Singers for the BBC. After, some years of small parish church choir work, including seven years Salford Choral Society… four concerts per season – Oratorio, *Messiah*, Oratorio, G&S. World-class soloists – Ian Partridge, D'Oyly Carte et al. – and the only society, other than the Halle, to perform in the Free Trade Hall, Manchester. Eight years St Ann's Church Choir (50) – Ronald Frost principal organ/general Royal Northern College of Music and chorus master to the Halle. St Ann's – all amateurs – sang *c.*25 matins/even-song and constantly broadcast for radio and TV… the latter included a 'live' matins.

Nine years Brick Church Choir, New York (20 – 15 pros, 5 volunteers) – David Weadon, also organist and choirmaster Princeton Theological Seminary. Five years Inverness Cathedral Choir – including two years Inverness Choral Soc. for two concerts per season. Four years St Mary's Ross-on-Wye (a cappella evensong no problem) and Gloucester Cathedral Choral Soc. – Andrew Nethsingha organist and choirmaster. The Bach Choir of Northampton – Andrew Reid, organist and choirmaster to Peterborough Cathedral.

Apart from concert halls and numerous specialist parish churches, the above have included performances in Cartmel Priory, Chester Cathedral, Gloucester Cathedral, Hereford Cathedral, Manchester Cathedral (also sometime summer choir for evensong),   Magdalen College, Oxford, York Minster, Princeton College Chapel, Temple Emmanuel NYC. Also include broadcasts for the BBC, Granada TV, WNCN NY and a performance with Dave Brubeck.)

The last was a real heady mixture! There we were draped round the chancel in Mexican costume and I was sitting three feet away. His massive concert grand was backed by three sidemen, including two sons, and a real live marimba band down by the conductor for ethnic fills and effects. Brubeck's composition was written around a traditional Mexican mass based on 'La Posada', the sixteen days' run-up to Christmas. This develops during the ceremony into 'La Pinata' –

symbolic of bread from heaven, hung in a big bundle in the centre of church or home, to be attacked by children at the appropriate moment with long poles. The Brick Church children were involved, also in native Mexican costume and choreographed by a member of the choir, who had sometime lent his knowledge to Broadway musicals. Brubeck's extended 'piano only' breaks were a great complement to our singing, and the children's enthusiasm in scrabbling around after the sweets which tumbled to the floor all added to the overall ambience of this wonderful performance.

I don't like listening to large orchestral concerts or big-scale opera... bored stiff. Give me the small group specialists, either instrumental or vocal. I once went to a serious ballet; *Swan Lake* featuring Margot Fonteyn and Rudolf Nureyev, who had come over to Manchester from Paris especially for the occasion, in the process pushing out a senior Covent Garden principal. Close inspection through my opera glasses showed that he had not just come over for the dancing!

True musical funny... I was there. A visiting German maestro taking a US choir trying to sing in German. (viz. nicht, ich, etc.) 'Nisssht, viishht, isshht... eet ez like zee warter cuming owt of zee taaps... or as you Americans say zee fowhcets. Pleeeze stopp ziss imeediately, or I go home now.' And he slammed his baton down on the music stand!

Maybe this is the appropriate chapter to clear up the Religion bit. My general exposure to the countryside, behavioural patterns in horses and dogs, peacocks regrowing perfectly symmetrical tails from nought to six feet in four months, tells me that something is happening outside our ken. We are just encouraged to take part and work with it, and nowhere is like the choir stall to observe where 'two or three are gathered together', and assess how the trend is going. Sadly it sometimes looks like that.

Answer: as far as the Anglican Church is concerned, going backwards and fast. Ducking people in water, playing bongo drums, camping out in a tent on the chancel floor in York Minster, and trying to mix politics and the pulpit – starring the new Archbishop of York – will not work. The better the show more people come and it's 'church' not theatre they're after. I am currently confusing the Archbishop of Canterbury with Father Christmas talking in a contrived Noel Coward accent. Surely from a bona fide Welshman we should be getting samples of 'boyo, yacky dah, look you' and others.

Why is *Choral Evensong* on Wednesday afternoons the longest-running BBC radio slot? Why is *Songs of Praise* the longest-running TV programme? The former happens most days in all our big cathedrals, also four times a week at St Thomas's 5th Avenue NYC – and what a choir! They even have a choir school and a Brit as the choirmaster, John Scott (ex-St Paul's), who has recently taken over from Gere Hancock. Their congregation is noticeably larger than St Paul's... it's all a question of quality, and then good products sell but need selling. (A little leaflet in Inverness Cathedral increased our evensong numbers and also the summer visitors' tea room take very substantially... what a good idea.)

Incidentally over 75% of the US attends a Christian church service on a Sunday, although there are only some two million 'Piskies'. A prominent US Episcopal Bishop told me that intelligence gathered from face-to-face meetings with the Pope, Archbishop of Canterbury and the Patriarch of the Orthodox Church could only describe the Islamic pressure on the world as 'mind blowing'. One can't get better Christian intelligence than that!

Muslim discipline certainly gets everybody co-ordinated. BUT, punishing a hungry 8-year-old child for stealing by publicly running over his little arm in the street, nicking infants' heads with a sword causing blood to pour over their faces (two pictures we cannot show), bullying the womenfolk, arranged marriages... NO, NO, NO!

We can and must be accommodating, but don't have to go to the extremes of changing the positioning of the loos in prisons to satisfy Muslims (25% of Brixton Gaol for one, and who have disobeyed the Koran to get there in the first place) from not facing Mecca whilst they are 'doing the nuisance'... this is a real live Indian one and said in your best oriental Peter Sellers!

The Christian Church might consider amalgamating around happily married vicars, priests and even bishops... it's a family affair. Singletons can, of course, work and contribute to the system in more individual roles such as deans, ecclesiastical dons and specialist overseas activities.

As I have observed, Holy Communion and Mass have been manoeuvred closer and closer over the past twenty-five years. Why not incorporate the two and sing the settings... they are the same, what a surprise! Use the wonderful, but fading, English churches for both albeit acting as one. Flog off confessional boxes for firewood!

Condoms for everyone, free issue if required, particularly in AIDS plagued areas... no more 'holier than thou' from senior clergy. Another horrid coming up on the horizon: Avian Flu (that's the birds' bit) or perhaps, er ahem, we are going to take on Avian Aids? (is that the human bit? – see where it's happening).

A joke to get us back to earth. If you put a first class stamp on a French letter, does it make the mail come any quicker?

The fifth generation of this musical exposé, my son Philip, actually became professional. He showed great promise as a child and, as his mother had overlooked getting him registered for second-stage boarding school, I managed to get him set for Charterhouse on a token gesture of a music scholarship... luckily his work was also much above average. This was an ideal venue as Bill Llewellyn, who had now progressed to the top spot, was fanatical to promote music to all pupils. He reckoned to have 85%+ making a contribution.

This led to discoveries such as the Genesis rock band and on a more serious side such as Philip, who took up the organ, became an ARCO (Associate of the Royal College of Organists) whilst still at school, got the FRCO the day he left, and progressed to Cambridge as the organ scholar to St John's College under George Guest. He served three years in this role and turned professional thereafter.

He played recitals extensively all around the UK, also overseas in Europe and the US. The latter were particularly entertaining for me in New York… nothing like throwing the *New York Times* in to an over-sleeping performer with 'There's a good review on page twelve. Bernard Holland on your performance at St Bart's on Tuesday.' I also enjoyed going to listen, and for one performance I laid on an oversize screen in the church so that all could see. (How many times have you actually seen the organist in action, feet and all?) We also got to know George Guest and his wife Nan, not only when they visited with the St John's choir, but also on other trips when he was taking choral workshops. Once we had all the St John's clerks to dinner, literally 'singing for their supper' with marvellous unaccompanied madrigals and funny songs. [b19]

However, it became a question of 'the loneliness of the international organ recitalist' and PCK retired… to become a successful director of a firm of private client stockbrokers!

Perform, perform, perform… it all comes through in the gut, and natural balance, finely tuned ear and 'charisma' (a real ghaastly one) make for mimicry, story telling and reciting. This can lead to 'you should have gone on the stage'. Well, I never tried, but on a number of occasions I have acted as producer.

Early 1980s a great friend, John Bromley-Davenport, who has become a successful barrister to the level of a QC, adapted Dickens'

Christmas Carol for a solo performance. He had the family acting bug, and had access to his uncle's fine private theatre at Capesthorne in Cheshire. I encouraged him to embellish the evening with a small, high quality choir to sing carols as the audience came in and during the interval. The latter was in the great hall of the house which, coupled with Christmas trees twenty feet high and footmen serving mince pies and mulled wine, all made for a very sophisticated evening.

The next year I had moved to New York, so we went transatlantic and I arranged a theatre at the Marymount School in the centre of Manhattan, as much audience as possible, and of course a choir. We also performed in the Union Club, and John was able to encourage family relatives out in New Jersey to put on a benefit performance.

Well, the following year we did it again, and this time his two daughters came with his wife, Judy, and her recently widowed father. A great time was had by all, and John canned a performance for Channel 5 TV. This was shown amongst mega national stars on their Christmas Day seasonal variety show... yes, he's as good as that!

This century I have organised some senior carol services for charities, three years in Hereford Cathedral and one in Brixworth Parish Church, Northamptonshire, dated AD 680. This involves picking up a scratch choir of thirty, set up on cathedral balance, and singing more unusual anthems and carols, often unaccompanied. Such a programme, coupled with mainly secular readings, makes for a very moving performance... all on three hours' rehearsal, so picking the choir is crucial.

A giant screen in Gloucester Cathedral in 2004, on behalf of the Acorns Children's Trust (hospice for small ones), further satisfied the organ fix, not only for the benefactor, but also some 250 others... so much better than twenty, staring into a dark, freezing cold abyss, on a very hard seat!

But where did it all come from for me? Answer; through grandfather

Charles Kenyon actor/manager, who can be researched on your internet under 'kenyon actors and actresses', where his name will be apparent. The following paragraphs, contributed by me for the Noel
Coward website, are a description of Kenyon's activities from the start
of the First World War.

In 1915 Kenyon was commissioned into the Hampshire Regiment and
was on active service until Armistice in 1918. This tour of duty took
him overseas, firstly to Gallipoli, and then considerable time was
spent in Egypt. He returned to his country home in Surrey with an
'Egyptian donkey'. Felly (named after the fellah) was a donkey/zebra
cross. They had been bred specifically for donkey stamina and zebra
speed, and were used for pulling ammunition tenders and light field
guns. Felly survived until the late 1940s.

January 1919 it was back to the stage, appearing at the New Theatre,
the Duke of York's, the Garrick, touring with his own company and
producing shows. It was the last, in conjunction with a well-respected
impresario, Alban Limpus, that *The Vortex* came to the West End. *The
Vortex* had been written, directed by and starred Noel Coward (with a
certain John Gielgud as an understudy, later to move into the title
role) and this move, on Coward's own admission at the time of his
75th birthday celebrations in the British media, was his first 'big
break'. The show opened in December 1924 and ran for a total of 224
West End performances. At the time of the opening Kenyon was
playing in *Blue Peter*, again produced by himself in conjunction with
Limpus. Before the run of *The Vortex* ended Kenyon and Limpus
approached Coward for the rights to *Hay Fever* as a vehicle for Marie
Tempest. She had previously turned the part down but Kenyon was
able to persuade her to re-consider and the play was produced at the
Ambassadors, directed by Coward. Alongside this euphoric two years
as a producer/manager Kenyon kept up West End appearances till his

final professional part in *The Strugglers* in July 1926 at the Scala theatre.

Charles Kenyon, the second of five children, started with the advantages of wealth, handsome looks and a fine deeply toned voice. This was particularly suitable for 'ultra English' roles so prevalent at the time. In 1902 he married Helen Statter, whose father was agent for the Earl of Derby, and they had three sons. After returning from the Great War however, Kenyon drifted from his family and spent time in several affairs with prominent female socialite and stage personalities. He spent time at the Savage Club, which still has a serious literary/stage membership, and enjoyed recreations of fox-hunting and tennis. He was always very well turned out for every occasion and was known as one of the best dressed men in London. First night dinners at The Caprice were standard fare, and his transport included a yellow Buick which was unusual for the UK. He died in Minehead Somerset after celebrating his golden wedding. This was considered strange by some, as he had not actually lived with his wife for some thirty years, although they met, weekended and corresponded regularly. [b20]

Hey… this all sounds a bit familiar… what are these gene things?!

9 All that Jazz

'For all the musicians in the house we'll jump the Muskrat Ramble'
(Armstrong)

It would be fair to say that I go from King Oliver to Monk – traditional, blues, swing and small group modern – coming to a halt for original sound no later than 1960.

The early melodies based on four-part harmony of treble (clarinet) alto (trumpet), tenor (trombone) and bass (tuba), supported by a rhythm section of banjo and drums, closely relate to four-part church music: thus easy to listen to and closely identifiable by church choir choristers, and those with athletic balance and timing built into the system. (Why are all the athletic track and field teams now predominately black? Answer; they have gifts of longer-legged/different body physique coupled with balance and the underlying sense of rhythm.) The same goes for black musicians who, albeit they were often only semi-literate at best in the beginning, were able to instinctively form a tune, and extend it into a harmonic progression, supported by a sense of timing. Later education brought out further abilities, but there has always been a double standard of highly trained versus those playing by ear and little else. Ellington could arrange/score away from any form of musical instrument or tuning device, Basie could hardly read music and certainly never played from it. African rhythms, slaves, negro spirituals, red hot gospellers, 'I love to hear the darkies sing those Dixie melodees' – that's the basis whether you like it or not, and don't forget good music lasts.

From this fundamental background jazz developed (all in one paragraph!) and a natural extension progressed into music for dancing. Strict continual tempo adapted for different steps. This diversified in the middle part of the twentieth century – 1955/1975 – when the whole concept shifted to rock, twists and other non-partner-contact dances, leaving the jive as the last link with the past. Does fundamental change in popular music taste affect human behaviour? Look over the last two centuries for starters through all levels of society. My early exposure gave me a split of fun jazz appreciation, and music for dancing in which I could participate.

My first serious jazz record was an Extended Play (45 rpm), one up in diameter of the modern CD, and two tunes on each side. This could be played on our 'radiogram' the forerunner of the music centre. The artists: the Benny Goodman Quartet – Goodman (clarinet), Lionel Hampton (vibes), Teddy Wilson (piano), Gene Krupa (drums). Four world-class musicians in their own right, who sometime led their own bands, and all of whom I saw subsequently performing. The combination of Wilson playing as a guest with the Lionel Hampton Orchestra at Carnegie Hall in 1988 was vintage stuff, both men in their eighties still performing at top level. One could go on expounding on marvellous evenings either in the concert hall or the more intimate atmosphere of clubs… some more memorable than others.

I was lucky to catch Louis Armstrong on the final lap of his real career… playing the trumpet. After the early 1960s he had the good sense to admit to lip deterioration and increased his own style of singing solo, until his death in 1971. This shift made more money relatively than he had earned since his early days with his original Hot

Five and Hot Seven bands. Venue: Manchester and the Armstrong All Star band which had toured Europe on a number of occasions. The line-up consisted of star musicians in their own right including Edmund Hall, Billy Kyle and Trummy Young. We had a stage box and were right in on the action. Satch walked in from our side to lots of banter and conversation, and so did the singer in a silver-sequinned mermaid dress so tight that she had to shuffle on to the microphone. We tried to get her to sing sitting on the side of the box... much to the amusement of the band.

Next stop the Victoria Palace London, Count Basie. Velvet curtain rises to band starting out on their first number, plum-coloured dinner jackets and white flannel trousers. Left stage on comes the 'Count', light grey sharkskin suit and cream silk shirt, grins at the audience, sits sideways, twiddles a few notes into the theme which is really getting warmed up and away he goes... conducting with occasional hand gestures. I saw him again, amongst other occasions, playing in the Starlight Roof on the top of the Waldorf Hotel NY. This was more a cabaret style concert, and at the invitation of 'whah don' y'all get up and dannce' we did!

Ellington concerts always seemed more formal... maybe there was a more disciplined attitude from the 'Duke'. I never met him, but had conversations with an English organist and choirmaster living in New York, Alec Whitin, who had befriended him and arranged the logistics and musical content for his funeral in New York Cathedral.

Club jazz in the 1960s was still quality. Jimmy Ryan's at West 52 St NYC was a mecca for the older stagers from early days, as was Eddie Condon's own club. I attempted to visit the latter in 1968 only to be met with a note on the basement entrance door: 'Sorry, boys, decided to retire, see you all in Jamaica.' Basin Street East was primarily a show club, a week at which was an essential on any big touring star's annual calendar. The club was always packed, and I will never forget fighting my way down the steps to watch Peggy Lee performing.

My very first night in New York in 1960, it was the venue for Benny Goodman with five sidemen and special guest Red Nervo. The last was a vibraphonist who had also played with Goodman in quartet days as an alternative to Hampton. A hastily penned note for a request which was granted: 'Whispering', one of the tracks on that first EP!

The ballrooms also featured serious jazzmen, arranging their presentations for both dancing and listening. Panama Francis (& his Savoy Sultans) summed it up: 'My feeling has always been that if you can't dance to it, it's not jazz.' Today the clubs, principally the Blue Note, Sweet Basil and Jazz Standard, present lower budget evenings, albeit high quality trio and quartet style of playing. Saxophonist Illinois Jacquet was an unexpected feature at Jazz Standard in 2002 – aged 80 and shortly before he died.

In the US I've always 'taken it in' wherever, including in a taxi in Chicago. The driver, an enormous chatty black, had three flutes parked up on the top of the dashboard and I noticed his fine long-fingered hands. Closer questioning showed that 'ahhve played wid 'em all man, Monk, you name it.' What a find. I paid up and listened to this prodigious talent practising with the 'Not on duty' sign on display!

The UK, sans the strong black undercurrent, never developed jazz in earlier days. American jazz form was extended into dance bands and often numbers to match. Orchestras of a dozen upwards were not uncommon, led by such leaders as Roy Fox, Harry Roy, Geraldo, and Sid Phillips. They also had a market on the radio. 'Big bands' developed from the US likes of Glenn Miller, Stan Kenton and Woody Herman. I, of course, never heard the first... and as for 'revival bands' without the original captain... ugh!

The trad revival from the US influenced such as Humphrey Lyttleton, Chris Barber, and bands from Europe such as the Dutch Swing College. However, outside the top few, who also managed to improvise commercial 'hits', the UK jazz scene has always been confined to the 'pubs and clubs' market – 100 Oxford Street, Ronnie Scott's – good fun, but not the same buzz and quality as the big staged occasion. Consider Kenny Ball, Chris Barber and Acker Bilk with their bands, together at the Barbican in 2006... um, er, perhaps? Oscar Peterson at an Albert Hall farewell concert on a warm June night in 2006... yes, yes! Give me Brubeck or the Dankworths any time for real wrinkly nostalgia. [b21] [b22]

A very small, private 'stage' is a black drum kit which sits in the corner of a certain study. This is for fantasy land only!

10 *Club Life*

'There is nowhere more felicitous than a seat in a good Club' (Dr Johnson)

Birds of a feather, the herding instinct, what you will; basically people like getting together, and as long as it's legally and morally acceptable, why the hell not. If you want the membership to be all men or all women, fine!

My first exposure to club life was a snapshot, breakfasting with Uncle at Boodle's crossing London on the way home from school. Russell, the head porter, had been briefed early on for 'now if you're in London and get stuck, just call Russell, I'm sure he can sort it out.' I never did but I'm sure he could have.

I graduated to membership of the Lansdowne compliments of Granny for my twenty-first birthday. She promised to pay the sub till she died, but must have had some intuition as this lasted only two years... she was kind but close. I had been elected to the MCC as a junior member (a great-uncle and his old Lancashire team crony, also a director of our company, were on the committee so it just meant signing a piece of paper – waiting list today seventeen years) and also the Manchester Tennis and Racquet Club.

The MTRC was a bastion of fun, as not only were there facilities for rackets and real tennis, but also there was a strong social fabric. Lunchtime collected the Manchester professionals and company owners, and some country based members just drifted in for the afternoon. The latter were a great catalyst for shooting, riding and other social events. The decanter flowed round the table, good-humoured 'fines' were imposed for passing it the wrong way or bringing in dud guests, a Stilton cheese was always on the table and another fine for scooping rather than slicing but… the place was falling to bits!

Two members, supported by some other enthusiasts, took the matter in hand and 'The Manchester Gold Racquet Weekend' was introduced. This was a forerunner of 'rackets and tennis weekends' as they have developed over the years, and was certainly organised with an eye to detail down to perfection. House parties for visitors, a Ball on Saturday night, magnificent lunches with cold grouse, fresh salmon, and oysters in the billiard room being shucked by a pro in his long white apron, all attracted the best players with girlfriends or wives. One year as 'weekend chairman' I organised the dance in the club with dancing in the rackets court. This required a quick turn-around from finishing games at 6 p.m. and being ready again for 9 a.m. the next morning. A clip-together dance floor was laid on carpeting and tables and chairs were placed around potted palm trees and shrubs which a member was able to supply from a stage set he had been organising up the road in a Manchester theatre. All candlelight completed the picture… sort of *Casablanca* nightclub stuff!

Backed by this new breath the club was still on its feet, but the fabric was years behind from the maintenance standpoint, and this all came to a head in the late 1970s, which happened to coincide with the centenary.

A very direct memo from a certain member on the committee not only caused virtual apoplexy amongst elderly members, but created the momentum to face the facts and do something. A group of four of us pushed and shoved, eventually all the far-reaching proposals were put in place, and the club has maintained its own individual presence ever since. But… the big question was, as usual, who will pay? Fundraising, generosity of some members, but it still needed the big one. Some years previously the same memo writer was rumbling, and as a start had compiled a list of club possessions.

Behind the door in the bar was an oil painting which, although obviously depicting a real tennis scene, was covered in the usual bar room grime. 'This is probably the best possession we've got.' The painting, by L. L. Boilly, was cleaned by Christie's, valued at £8,000 and hastily placed on loan to a Manchester art gallery. I suggested that we harness the painting and commission a limited edition (250) mezzotint print, not only as a memento to the Club Centenary, but also as a contributor to the development fund.

This project was great fun to organise, involving Lawrence Josset, one of the finest traditional engravers of all time, and the quaint printers and hand-colourers. The buyers who 'garaged' some copies have been well rewarded – present day value c. £1,500. I also undertook to write and manage the sale of a short club history (350), which again has increased in value to £200. [b23] This was published in a hardback, enabling members to subscribe from their businesses… at the exorbitant rate of £1,000 per page. However, we were still short of our fund goal and so the goose (original painting) was sold at Christie's for £58,000… problem solved!

My sojourn in the US had me enrolled as a member of arguably two of the finest men's clubs in the world – The Racquet & Tennis Club and The Union Club. Sports and social, 1,000 and 75 yards from my front door respectively. The former was predominately focused on racquets (their spelling so not to get confused with 'the rackets' i.e. Al Capone) and court tennis. These had a back-up of a wet area, incorporating a swimming pool and steam room, a billiard room, and squash courts. The last included a doubles court. This absorbing game also featured at the Union with the larger court, comfortably accommodating four people, and a hard black ball.

Both clubs have excellent dining and library facilities – the R&T with one of the finest collections of sporting books and the Union one of the largest private libraries in the world. The Union is not a mixed membership, but ladies are welcome to the extent that widows can still use the club for lunch, and wives can pledge husband's credit. At the R&T women have to wait in the 'strangers' room' by the porter's desk! Rooms at the Union and a reciprocal right with Boodle's meant that I occasionally used the latter when in London: 'what the hell are you doing in here, Kenyon, very offside.'

I just love dining in the Boodle's ladies' section as the guest of a serious financier's widow… ex-MI6 (aka 003), trilingual, *Times* crossword no problem… a sophisticated English woman at her best. 'Like fine wine, they just get better as they get older', as volunteered by a 'sporting' friend now deceased… how true!

No bedrooms at the R&T, but always cover at the desk from Tom, now retired and living in Florida. 'I'll just check and see if he's in the Club, madam'… knowing perfectly well that you were, or were not, by looking at the name board behind him, and then taking the temperature with the member in question. Selection for senior US clubs, social or sporting, is on a two-tier system. First the 'green light committee' to see if you are even fit to be considered, hopefully graduating to the full membership committee for election, supported by letters and references.

Currently my London club 'membership' is with the Savile Club and the Lansdowne… through the MTRC and the Tennis & Rackets Association. NYC nil!

The T&RA, which runs out of The Queen's Club, is currently under threat. The two rackets and tennis courts could be converted to crèches for children if some oikocrat or other buys the entire complex.

We all originally thought 'development' was to build a few houses – bad enough. But oh no, develop the lawn tennis and create gyms and spas for a leisure business – I can hardly believe that I'm writing this.

The Savile is a delightful look into the past featuring fine downstairs rooms and a panelled bar; upstairs a ballroom is reached by colonnade stairs and doubles as the mixed dining room. The bedrooms, although getting modernised, still have a sharing bathroom routine for some, and the genteel shabbiness chic of a substantial country house. A board indicates that 'Conversation is discouraged at the breakfast table'. Your 'good morning' is greeted by a few grunts and rustling of newspapers, indicating that your fellow breakfasters are at least still alive. Further ordering and instructions with the steward are conducted in whispers. The Lansdowne, recently refurbished, is a landmark of art deco furnishings and design... still featuring the squash courts, vast swimming pool and a fencing court!

Golf clubs should be run by one person who knows exactly what's what, delegating any special experience required to the right member who can provide the answer. I was a member of such a club, albeit there was a token committee, to cover the boundaries of democracy. The one gap in the secretary's most efficient modus operandi was a certain propensity to 'making do'. A little roll bag containing a few clubs and carried under his arm, and a fine spaniel as a companion, all contributed to serious single handicap golf well into his seventies, and never having to buy a golf ball. Occasionally he would tuck a .410 shotgun into the bag and shoot a few rabbits during his customary very early morning stroll round the course. You have to find the right person for this sort of approach, such as old Wykehamist Tony Legard. He was affectionately known as 'Loopy', and died six months ago aged 82. Nevertheless, we still had to have a serious memo to upgrade the clubhouse facilities, even though this club hosts British Open qualifiers when the tournament is on the Lancashire coast.

Becoming 'captain' of the club can transcend certain individuals into a dizzy height of extreme self-importance; the ladies can be even worse (with their big tweed-trousered golfing bums... sorry girls, even the finest tailors cannot solve the problem, try a skirt) and as for lifetime 'presidents'! A golf club is a golf club where one plays golf, not a social melting pot.

Golf in Scotland still has a more 'golf, a drink, a good lunch, and home' approach at all their wonderful courses. I was a member of two and have played many, particularly the lesser known... these can be better than the greats. The latter have apparently become very much in demand for the tourist, but with some careful planning a tee time can now usually be arranged to suit, even at so-called peak periods... could it be that there are fewer tourists?

And then there were the other kind of clubs... opening say 10 p.m. onwards. Live music, good floor show, fair play tariff, and yes, you had to be a member. The Blue Angel, The 400, The Society were one thing... Murray's, The Stork Room and Churchill's were another. Even some dance clubs, such as Edmundo Ros, featured discreet notices such as that 'hostesses' or 'dance partners' were available. There is still one such club in the West End and, although the same vintage, it's not featured above. Sorry to say that modern day equivalents with disco music, relatively over-priced drinks and very mixed social clientele are not even at the starting line. Who wants to see a load of polo-playing puppy doggies puking all over the pavement?

11 Parties

All usually have a focus, and a mixture of activities are the best variety. This equally applies to the weekend house kind, going away for jolly hols en groupe or just a good old 'bash'.

I always refuse the rare kind offers of sitting on a motor yacht for more than an afternoon. Hell on earth, regardless of the bikinied furnishings and 'yacht lizards' – one worse than the 'lounge' model. The sailing boat variety are tremendous, providing the craft are over 50 ft and one can just sit and watch the hilarious comedy which unfolds... no spinnakers, winching, going about, for me. Each to their own!

In early days the Hunt Ball provided for a good catalyst and on a certain occasion I found myself in Oxfordshire. My hosts' daughter was firmly in the sights of an old school pal, Myles, and a coterie of friends had been gathered for the event, some going 'steadier' than others.

Everybody, bar Myles and self, was into the fox-hunting aspect of things and I got off to a slow start at the dinner party on Friday evening. Just a few extra friends turned out to be couples of Mum and the Commander's vintage, and the conversation was about nothing but the horse... non-stop. Nothing like talking to two attractive backs for a couple of hours, as obviously I was not 'one of us'. This was further elaborated at the port stage when, feeling rather puckish, my response to 'Well do yah ride at all, Kenyon?' was 'Oh yes sir, a 500cc Norton and it goes rather well.' I later heard, 'funny fella that Kenyon, he rides a motorcycle.' More inclusive was: 'Where d'yah come from, Nigel?' 'Er, Cheshire, sir.' 'Cheshire eh... gad nowhere like it, all sex and saddle soap.' So my stock had gone up... just.

Saturday morning the luckless pair declared that they did not wish to go to the meet, but maybe could flight some pigeons in the afternoon. I had noticed obvious signs of shooting around the house which stood overlooking fine valleys leading down to the river Thames. This was met with 'no guns available', but was reversed when I was able to produce one from my car (always have one with you just in case) and, after all, Myles was dating the daughter. We set off, having been briefed about the pheasant coverts – 'only shoot the odd one out of the hedges' – and a few shots later we already had a small bag of various.

A shot, 'I've got it,' and almost immediately surrounded by hounds, put me on high alert. Surely not a fox... only semi-fortunately not, as some tooting horns down by the river confirmed men in breeches and green jackets but no horses or our hosts! This was the Christchurch College Beagles, and Myles had shot the hare in front of the pack which had crossed the river out of control of the huntsman. Luckily not seen, we bagged the hare, hounds were called back and we headed for home. The lights were beginning to twinkle up at the big house and I had noticed a pheasant roosting situation starting in a spinney of poplars. Myles was placed accordingly for some excellent shooting at the bottom of the valley as I drove them out from the top.

On the hunters' return we were happily ensconced with tea in the drawing room. Slightly scathing, 'Well, did you get anything?' 'Yes,

Philip graduates from Cambridge

The stockbroker on his penthouse terrace

The Worshipful
Company of
Feltmakers – Dining at
The Mansion House

With German
aristocracy

Father Christmas
comes to supper

On de Nile

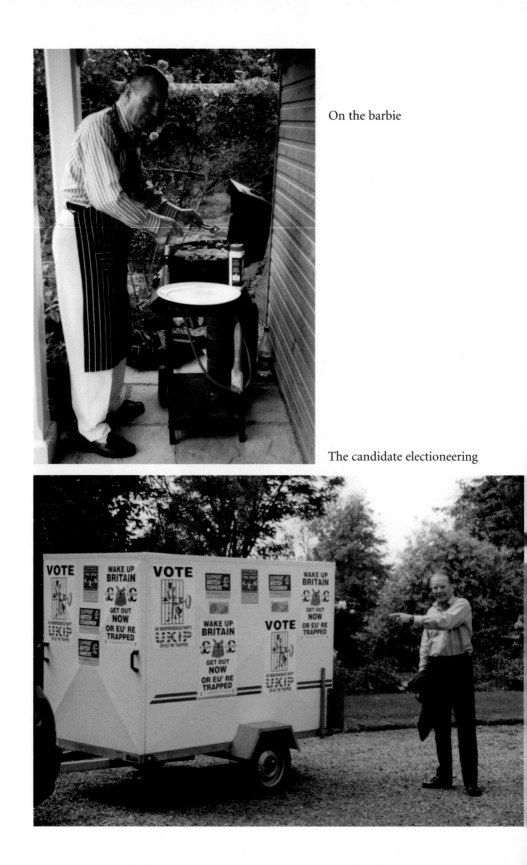

On the barbie

The candidate electioneering

Our safety is in our speed

Kenyon in Kenya with Kenyans

ON SAFARI

Riding the range

Consulting the committee

Too many
cooks?

The dining
room

With members of The Royal Ascot
Racing Club

'Owners & Trainers' – The Derby
2005

Going a bit loony

The Meadow Club – Southampton, Long Island

The Inverness Cathedral Choir visiting Magdalene College, Oxford

thank you, we had great fun. Cook told us to put them all on the table in the larder.' Them was in fact eighteen units, predominately pheasants and the Christchurch hare. Our hostess declared that this was 'maahhvellous' and the rest of the evening was a rip-roaring success. An old Colonel – he really was – told me years later whilst watching a hunting exercise in front of my lodge, 'young or old these gals get really jazzed up after a day's hunting'… must be the air!

Unusual guests are always memorable, like returning from the races en groupe for Saturday night dinner and stay. 'Oh, I forgot to tell you that one of Mummy and Daddy's people is staying for the weekend.' Now it transpired that 'people' were the focus of serious rehabilitation for criminals prior to release from the local prison. On arrival 'person', in smart suit and cream shirt, was sitting in the large medieval drawing room reading the paper. He progressed with the rest of us through drinks and into dinner, and wound up sitting next to me… probably best to be all matter of fact?

'I hear you're, er, on leave.'

'Yes absolutely, I'm actually out from prison for the weekend. One more month and then I'm probably going to retire. You see I'm a burglar and, although they are watching me, they will never find the goods… and don't worry, the owners could afford it. First time I've been caught, and I've been at it most of my life.'

'Oh, and to what do you attribute your success?' I was then briefed that you worked on your own, no support such as drivers and fences, and only high quality targeted subjects, above all no weapons or violence.

Locked out in the garden of the substantial mansion, protected by locks, bolts, chains and shutters, all 'obstacles' were navigated in a matter of a few minutes and there he was snapping on the lights back in the drawing room. 'Alarms take longer and require more rehearsal.' Perhaps he made another fortune on the Costa del Somewhere, I have not taken his instructions any further than theory!

Singing for one's supper can mean literally or in various roles, such as miming, acting, playing backgammon, or that four of bridge. What a wonderful game... but, oh that one could play at 11 o'clock in the morning when we are all – including birds and animals – at our best. Ten p.m. onwards I am certainly not, and as for that 'I've got second wind' at 2 a.m. dancing an eightsome reel... oh no you haven't, you're propped up on stimulus, maybe alcohol or even, er, carnal excitement, the rest of you is fast asleep. However, having to listen to one's host was a must do, taken to memorable proportions if one wanted to maintain favour and continue paying court to a certain, unusually striking, red-headed daughter.

After dinner, instead of sitting round the table, the men were invited to our host's grand study from where, as a prominent psychiatrist, he administered two mental hospitals. One, general purpose, was at the bottom of the park which surrounded their fine Georgian home, the other a few miles away, of a more private nature – gentlemen lunatics.

We were subjected to various discussions, stimulated by the port or whisky decanter, and it could be that he was 'on duty' and one could be invited to don a white coat and go off with him on his rounds... gulp!

He was also on call to the Government and was asked to give his opinion on the behavioural patterns of a variety of individuals, sometimes visiting dignitaries. This could take place when he was included at a reception, a dinner or merely mingling with the crowd. It was from this that we learned that Nikita Khrushchev, then President of Communist Russia, was a serious manic-depressive. 'Now he's okay, but I'm going to Washington next week to monitor his state visit, he could be in a manic mood by then.' Very alarming stuff, when one considered that Mr K had a war-crimes record as long as you name it, and would probably have been executed at the end of the Second World War except for being on the 'winning side'. He always travelled overseas with Nikolai Bulganin as an escort (Mr B & Mr K) who had to control tantrums and other behaviour which never reached the public domain, other than to a select few after a delicious dinner. Mind boggling! [b24]

Recently a well-known society friend [b25] came out with 'we were lucky, Nigel, living through the second half of the last century for all those parties as we grew up'. Being a bit nostalgic maybe, wishful thinking, anno domini creeping along? I don't think so… they were better, and modern efforts rarely match, unless the hosts know the ropes. Mr & Mrs Nouveaux Richards are sometimes reluctant to learn, or try and emulate their 'young' (ugh! this one ties for first place with 'kids'), and they certainly don't know!

As the great party-givers do know, one never gives the same party twice, i.e. hardy annuals are very boring. Good bashes always have a theme, a different venue or variable style of music… music and lighting are the key to a successful dance party. The former must be live and adaptable, particularly for a mixed age group of adults. Yes, dancers want contact, particularly those who can dance. Bopping around waving one's hands in the air is for the nobrainers, which includes celebs trying to draw attention to themselves, others who can't tie a bow tie, and therefore don't wear one, or those who drink out of bottles.

Our band therefore should have a variety of instruments that enables sections to play a certain style or even be left on their own whilst the rest take a break. Amplification should be kept to the minimum of an odd microphone for singing or solo instrumental work, and no electronics please, other than maybe an acoustic guitar. Real musicians don't need them… nor do the guests! Discos are a cheap (excuse me, inexpensive) copout. Sad to say these are becoming more prevalent… your party's going to be expensive, get the main ingredient right.

One friend, John, had it right with Humphrey Lyttleton leading his band from the corner of the dining room – smallish band, big dining room. I had it right with a six piece trad line up, which could also play anything, for a party entitled 'The Roaring Twenties'. A quasi-cousin, Victoria, call me Plum, had it right at her debutante party with Bobby Harvey leading the band and singing from the piano. Their private ballroom was humming and so was Harvey, unfortunately singing himself into oblivion to the accompaniment of champagne being swigged from a bottle, the dolly tub under the piano bearing witness to quantity. The Viscount – her father – was standing getting redder in the face than his hunting-pink evening coat: 'Just what does this fellow think he's doing?' Well, Harvey answered the question momentarily by passing out on the keys… the Viscount closed the party forthwith. Like many night owl entertainers and jazzmen, the highly talented Bobby Harvey destroyed himself through drink. Being put on the milk train, asleep amongst the mail sacks, at 5 a.m., with a label round your neck 'Tired musician, please deliver the West End of London', cannot go on for ever!

Another great party entertainer in the 1960s, albeit rather at the end of his career, was Leslie Hutchinson (Hutch). [b26] He was a wonderful pianist with great natural touch and a deep-seated left hand on the lines of Fats Waller. He sang away, particularly to the ladies, and often in his cabaret round in London covered at least two venues per night. His style was continued and copied to effect by Bobby Short, who died only recently in New York. Short managed to galvanise a society following using the Carlyle Hotel as his base, but he never had the musicianship qualities of Hutch. 'Give us a song Hutch' across the bar at the Carlyle was met with his big goggle eyes out on stalks and mouth hanging open. Somebody knew of his secret mentor.

However, East Coast America still has it right with society bands such as Lester Lanin (the principal, recently deceased, was so ancient that he had to be 'wheeled out', but what a pro), Mike Carney, Peter

Duchin, Alex Donner and Bob Hardwick. With bandleader hats off they might easily be guests. Hardwick, an ex-stockbroker who conducts his band from the piano, has been flown over for a party in the UK shires, travelling East as it were. Donner just sings and exhorts his musicians with 'take it away, boys.' If you want something more traditional try Vince Giordano and the Nighthawks.

Now what happened to that invitation to a real 'Cocktail Party', properly made mixed drinks, thoughtfully presented wine, well-made canapés of substance, gals in silk dresses or tailored suits, fellas in well-cut kit, and hopefully never in two rooms, i.e. duds naturally congregating in one and les amusants in the other. Answer: drinks 6.30 p.m. or Sunday 12 noon; dress: smart casual. These get-offs are known in even polite US society as 'cluster fxxks'!

The record for this type of event must be 250 guests, at $100 a throw, 'and I can't fit another one in', obviously no more clusterables! However... 'A pleasure to meet you last weekend, Nigel. Now I need you for two consecutive evenings later this month.' Major 2006 summer season parties, given by a 'top 400' NY society hostess – get those white trousers pressed at once!

Brit versions have a tendency towards cheap wine, fake champagne and prunes wrapped in bacon – naturally referring to fruit.

The following appeared in a letter published in the *Field* magazine in 2004 in response to a contribution on how to make a Bloody Mary; we start with an alternative.

Bloody Mary – of a sort. Akvavit base – Aalborg for preference. Add 2/1 tomato to orange juice, latter preferably fresh and a good dash of Worcester Sauce. Shaken not stirred, of course. Yes, ice just goes in the shaker.
Gin & Tonic. No apology for going through this one. Often so badly presented at those ghaastly, street-sweep invites – 'drinks 12 noon'.

Ice surrounded by 4 slices of cucumber to large tumbler, pour on
spirit (it can be vodka, usually for the gals who prefer Vodka Marties)
add tonic and a light stir through. This is a different drink to 'would
you like ice and lemon' after the liquids have been poured into the
glass.
Pimms NB. Ice into jug first. NO fortification of basic mix with extra
spirit. Schweppes lemonade for preference. Only add sliced cucumber, mint and borage – if you have it. Tepid, treacly fruit salad in a
glass is quite disgusting!

Recently my hostess asked me if I'd like a Bloody Mary, 'I make a jolly
good one, just like they do in the States,' and promptly stuck a stick of
celery in the glass. Er, no your Ladyship, that's a bar in Nebraska at
best, and by the way the place is referred to as the United States...
merely thinking to myself, of course!

[See appendix 'Eating & Drinking' for other ideas.]

12 Across the Pond

'Uncle Sam and the Big Bagel' (Taki)

As I am currently solo and unlikely to live for another forty-five years, my longest lifetime love affair will be with the United States. Their big trump card, space, and this enables a mix of different races and styles of people to live together in a progressive harmonious manner. Once they get to know you and like you, your project, suggestion or whatever, there is an enthusiastic bubble to progress the matter in question. No routes, à la GB, of 'who will sponsor me', 'do we get a grant' and other forms of 'owt fer nowt'. In other words, the people direct America based on their own initiative.

My first night in 1960 got me straight into gear. I arrived off the plane from Montreal and straight to cousin Humphrey's apartment on Park Avenue. He (52), a divorced bachelor, was attractive and socially very much a man in demand. Sure enough he was entertaining a well-known socialite lady who immediately took me under her wing and 'you sit here with me.' She had a fleet of cars at a certain garage if I needed transport and, as her son was going to army camp that summer, 'I'm just going to write to those mothers who are giving parties for all those cute gals, and have them put you in Gilbert's place.' So debs' delight, or escort anyway, in twenty minutes and head beginning to swim after getting through the second Martini: 'just like your Uncle Terence used to make and never forget that no bird ever flew on one wing.'

We flew along to Basin Street East to take in some supper and Benny Goodman's first set, and then off out to the country where 'you're spending the weekend at my sister's'. Here I was greeted and introduced to the departing dinner/bridge group in one big whirl and ended up, well past midnight, fast asleep in my fine old Edwardian bedroom with matching colonial furniture. I was suddenly awakened by 'good night', 'call me next week' and the retreating car on the gravel drive. Five minutes later, tap tap tap on the door and female voice: 'Nigel, come down to the kitchen immediately.' Now I had forgotten that 'my sister (Frances) has a very attractive daughter'… and there she (Stella) was sitting at the table, bright blue eyes, long blonde hair, wrapped up in a feathery housecoat: 'Wow, so you're Nigel.'

The summer progressed by accompanying Frances and Stella out to Sioux City, Iowa, on their annual summer trek to see Granny (Old Stella), a widow, who had been married to Dyke Statter. (You remember the introduction, the family who had emigrated from Lancashire.) The trip was via the Mayo Clinic for annual medical check-ups – would I like one?… no thank you.

Sioux City was a real Midwestern experience. Review of family farms, visiting friends – several of whom had met an uncle out on a similar trip in the 1930s – digging for Red Indian artefacts and a private visit to the Sioux Reserve itself. Log cabins, the real thing wandering around and an old 'squaw' cooking cats for lunch! The contact was through the curator of the museum who himself was half Indian, and very onside for advising on the family collection of Indian antiquities and beadwork. The golf course had a good laugh when I used my umbrella to keep off the brutal sunshine, midnight swimming at the country club, water-skiing – for the first time, straight up and away – and barbecues were all a foretaste of things to come.

We returned via Chicago and visited the Republican Convention for the 1960 national election. Frances was a serious party worker and so we were able to watch from prime seats although we only had two tickets. But that did not seem to matter... so much for security.

I then attended some debutante parties as promised, and on several occasions found me in the main hostess's dinner party. Being summertime these were mainly out in the country, say on Long Island at such venues as Seawanhaka Yacht Club and Piping Rock at Locust (aka Lowco$t) Valley. The latter is a year-round residential hideout for prominent Long Island families who can continue to enjoy all forms of sporting activity yet still be comparatively close to NYC.

And so to Fishers Island. It was customary for Humphrey to take a house for the month of August for the family, their friends and other houseguests. This large Cape Cod seaside house just fitted in so well for all the fun going on at Fishers.

The Island is situated a short ferry ride off New London, Ct. No hotels or public places to stay, and woe betide if you let your house to a dud. The area is split into two by a guarded gate on the main road – still a modest sort of lane – which runs through the middle. On the north end is the golf course, country club and beach club, at the ferry end a nine-hole course and the Hay Harbour Club which has a serious tennis and children's emphasis. So... it was virtually all private and it still is today! Breathtaking scenery, wildlife galore, you can sit underneath osprey nests all day if you wish, smaller beaches, some very grand old summer houses. The main golf course is world class scenically... actual quality as a course, debatable as usual.

After all this hectic 'summer stuff' I had to return to Canada for something called work. I managed to squeeze in one more trip to the US, and this time also went up to Harvard to meet France's son Dykie. He was studying something and what a great fellow. He had a natural magnetism which drew all the 'sportsmen' around him, and a good time was had by all… and some!

For the next twenty years or so I visited the US for just a variety of reasons as illustrated in other parts of the story. One particular visit included a trip south to Salt Creek Ranch, Refugio, Texas. Salt Creek (60,000 acres) is part of the O'Connor complex which totals some 850,000 acres… just a few less than the King Ranch.

This low-key fortune runs on family lines, supported by cattle and oil. John Tatton's father, Jack, was the undergraduate friend of my father mentioned in our music chapter. He married Virginia O'Connor, moved to Refugio and only visited GB twice ever again. He ran things from a study bungalow in the garden, which had been built out of imported Derbyshire stone… to remind him of home! A fireplace, chintz covers and a Bechstein piano completed the picture. Help in the house included Nelson, the black butler ('How are you today Nelson?' 'Ahm okay, Mistah Kenyon… at least I think ah am. See, I've been oreful sick recent. But ahm bettah terday.' What a fine man.) and Dolores, the housekeeper who could iron like no one else. The hands outside lived in Mexican style cottages and everybody was fiercely loyal to the family. This was reciprocated with help and generosity… shades of the 'Mill', this time Tatton's of Leek!

My friends visited me, as newly wed couples, as single ladies, until in 1983, whilst on a trip introducing my Philip to the scene, I met Susan. Yes, you've guessed, at Fishers Island. I was staying in another gal's house, but she deserted me for 'urgent business in New York', leaving me to fend for myself. Big mistake!

After some transatlantic visits, I was on my way to live in Manhattan, February 1985. A new apartment had been bought for the occasion and there we were, 68th Street between Park and Lexington Avenues, the centre of the bull's-eye.

Life just worked. I had a service office for commerce, sometimes on assignment in other people's, clubs were within walking distance, as was all the other mainline focus of the great City.

Proper coffee shops have always fascinated me. Nothing like Neil's at 70th & Lexington, with Victor the waiter in full cry, dealing with a clientele varying from senior executives, to stage personalities, to call girls all intermingled with Noo Yawk in general. This in contrast to society-led eateries such as Elaine's, Swifty's (aka Shifty's) and all the usual suspects. [r6] Decent men's haircuts are virtually impossible, always have been. We discovered Olga in a midtown salon; she has now graduated to the barber's shop at the St Regis Hotel.

Real tennis was enhanced outside the membership of the Racquet Club by being able to play out at Greentree, the home of the Whitney family. This was by invitation, including Bostwicks, Coreys et al., and was always for doubles on Saturday and Sunday mornings. The court was part of the house and was approached by a back staircase leading past the library. The latter not only housed a great collection of books but also paintings including a very substantial Toulouse Lautrec over the mantelpiece.

This venue was the stage for the Greentree Weekend in November when Betsy Whitney (Ambassador Jock's widow) hosted the weekend, including lunch in the library for all on both days. No social gaffes please, don't take a dud date, and fortunately a serious blunder by self went no further. I hailed a very elegant looking black man passing by – 'er, steward could you please bring me two Bloody Marys?' – who turned out to be our hostess's son-in-law. This was met with a very black look... as it were.

For summertime we travelled and had a glorious month at Fishers Island. Susan had been taking a house for a number of years and I soon got to know her friends and contacts. Only one diplomatic problem was around the beach club where I had to pay a fee each time I visited; we weren't married. I had some serious correspondence with the club president, mentioned membership of clubs in NYC and such things as the 'Nelsonian eye' in these matters, but he would have none of it. Porter Goss has recently been 'stood down' after less than two years as Director of the CIA in the current Bush administration. If in power at that time, he would probably have had me sent off to Guantanamo Bay with no remission for good behaviour. Nevertheless it was all fun, even at $5 a clip, but as a beach I prefer Isabella anyway!

Susan sometimes accompanied me on trips to GB and we always met up with friends in London and Cheshire. They were curious as to whether Americans understood me and my particular English (aka posh-sounding mumble – by some) accent. She had to admit that sometimes she didn't, to which she was told, 'well, don't worry, neither do we.'

Let's get this English speak, UK v. US stuff, sorted out. It's not the same, but at least we understand one another. Try your US – Clothes: suspenders, vests, garters, pants. Cars: hoods, fenders, trunks, mufflers. Restaurants: busboys, chow, jigger, captains. Body: ass, fanny, pecker, snatch. Translate either way, and smile! By the way fellow Brits, it's Hughston and Los Angelis – not who and lees. And please, after one trip to Disneyland or a package weekend to NYC, don't try 'guys, ballparks or rain checks'.

Susan and I had a common interest in music – she is an excellent amateur pianist – and this meant not only listening, but going together for choir at the Brick Presbyterian Church, where five of us volunteers blended in with fifteen professional singers.

The Brick runs as church should be run. We had a senior padre, Revd Dr Herbert Anderson (now retired), who was a marine, and he was supported by a lady, the Revd Leslie Merlin (now pastor of the Second Presbyterian Church in NYC). Yes, a lady vicar, happily married, had been divorced, with an attractive family. The extensive staff also served a junior day school for a cross-section of children.

This still all continues under new management, and recently a major refurbishment has been topped off by the installation of a magnificent organ. The previous model, a four-manual old warhorse, was 'coughing' but the budget, even at the Brick, was running out. A parishioner came to the rescue: 'please proceed and send me the bill'… $2.5 million worth, but that's America!

A big support for all this activity is my old friend Ellsworth Stanton. This international character still heads up major charities in NYC, is on friendly terms with the British royal family – such as friendship with the late Queen Mother, Ascot appearances and visits to Balmoral. He is a Knight of St John and has recently been awarded an honorary MBE, both as an American. His Scottish Munro ancestry brings out the kilt. Not all US Anglophiles arrived on the *Mayflower*. If such references were all collated, this good ship would have had a passenger list of many thousands!

When in town at the weekend we sometime went cycling in Central Park, Susan on her old-fashioned Raleigh, me on my mountain bike. The latter was also used as fun transport around town, even down Park Avenue, and one Saturday I cycled all around the peripheral of Manhattan. This adventure gave one a very close look at a wide variety of situations, both behavioural and living conditions, and maybe was a prompt for a scheme I initiated whereby we collected sports and recreation equipment – good second-hand and new – for redistribution to needy community and church-based youth groups.

The idea quickly caught on, with support from the Department of Youth Services who were represented on the Mayor's main board, WNBC Channel 4 News and other press. In the first eighteen months some sixty groups had benefited throughout the five boroughs: the Bronx, Brooklyn, Queens, Staten Island and good old Manhattan. This included baseball equipment, roller blades, athletic clothing, shoes, racquets, you name it! A call to a friend, Gene Scott (Gene played in the Davis Cup as an amateur, was one of the finest sportsmen ever at Yale, but sadly died of a heart attack in 2006 aged only 68), produced 200 extra tennis racquets from the USTA to fill the gaps on our wish lists. This instance was coupled with a cold call to Flushing Meadow – home of the US Open – who supplied us with the two-week-old world-class nets from the last year's tournament... the following year they also sent the posts and massive cartons of balls! These ready-made packages quickly re-equipped old courts, and at least 800 children were exposed to tennis – dreams turned into reality. The USTA had spotters (GB please note) who even visited these very humble yards, and in the first year several youngsters were upgraded to serious coaching. The daily action at the Harlem Tennis Center, based in an old armoury, is another wonderful story, and often I was asked to attend the handover of equipment in situ.

A memorable occasion was leading a stream of youngsters up a very lowly street in Red Hook – the old dockland of Brooklyn – to four refurbished courts where tennis took place with at least five a side! This was filmed by Channel 4 outside broadcast, with who I hitched a ride back to the City... never forgetting the welcome air-conditioning of the van on one of the hottest days in July. The outside broadcast manager at the time was Geoff Scarborough, brother of Chuck, the nationally famous newsreader and sometime Southampton habitué.

Indoors, art departments were equipped, musical instruments were eagerly put to use... the list became endless. However the biggest bonus came in raising the awareness of volunteers who came in to help with coaching. (GB please note.) Amongst all the variety, there was a particularly memorable assignment when we helped re-equip a 'sanctuary' in the middle of Harlem.

This was a place where each afternoon at least 150 youngsters sought a warm play area after school, and even sometimes begged the charming warden and his wife not to be sent home. Having been asked to 'review the files' when I went personally to appraise the situation, I could see why. (I always did this wherever. Part of the education, and that particular occasion a cold, wet, January afternoon having been playing real tennis at the Whitneys' in the morning... quite a contrast!) He did admit that occasionally, knowing of the horrid situation at home, they had succumbed and taken drastic action the next day with the appropriate authorities.

Their wish list for gym equipment, a total art department, instruments, computer, table tennis tables and others was filled by March, including a sharp telephone call from, er, someone to another government department which resulted in decorating the changing rooms and refurbishing all the lockers. Handover evening was focused around a magnificent spread of sandwiches, cakes and trifles all prepared by parents of the dozens of eager black faces. The Director of Youth Services also happened to be in Harlem that evening, and joined us later on.

Tuesday, November 12 1991, House of Representatives, Hon. Hamilton Fish, Jr.

'Mr Speaker, I offer appreciation and praise to the many fine people I know who, over the years of severe government funding reductions, have selflessly volunteered for community service. One of these individuals, who is resident of New York City and part-time resident of my district, is Nigel Kenyon. Mr Kenyon has generously developed his time and efforts to the establishment of a citywide program to assist less fortunate young people. The program is designed to collect donated sporting equipment and distribute it to youth groups throughout the city. Mr Kenyon's endeavour has received tremendous support from local organisations and government agencies, as well as acclaim from Mayor Dinkins. I applaud Mr Kenyon for his contribution to his community. It is well deserved. His zeal and enthusiasm for community service is an inspiration to us all.'

The Congressional Record of the USA (11-13-91 E3821.)

However, they don't all work... as illustrated by an extract from a letter of mine – UK industry's parsimonious attitude to giving – published in the *Financial Times*, November 1990. This was in response to an article where 'Cathedrals are attracting new guardian angels' – i.e. industrial 'angels' sponsoring their choirs.

… Some 12 months ago I tried to extend an admirable fundraising drive being undertaken on behalf of Salisbury cathedral here in the US – by Americans be it noted.

As a Briton, now based in New York and continually ashamed of the one-way transatlantic begging bowl, my idea was to broaden the scheme to include Ely, Worcester and Hereford by canvassing British companies via their subsidiaries here in the US. Results were to be published in a certain newspaper, listing the names of donors if they so wished. Replies were received from more than three hundred head offices in the UK but, sad to say, contained all the old feeble excuses and only one cheque for $100. The whole exercise cost me my donation of $5,000…

End of story... except that the showpiece from the UK was supposed to be ex-Prime Minister Sir Edward Heath, who lived in the Salisbury Cathedral close and sometime postured as an organist. Yes, he would be delighted to come for the opening lunch but 'only travelled on the Concorde!' This was at the Union Club, where I was a member at the time, and I have never been as ashamed as watching this unsmiling, sweaty buffoon pompously expounding on his has-been self. Unfortunately he has to feature again in my political chapter.

The US operates on a switchback and the early 90s was down time. Susan had a daughter who had been brought up in NYC, where it's the same whether you are in a public school or at a posh variety, say Chapin or Spence for the girls, Buckley or St Bernard's for the boys. School stops at 3 p.m.... enough said.

She had moved to a college down south in Charleston and was strongly promoting mum to join her for warmer weather, great cultural activities, but 'this does not include Nigel'. I had done my best, but second-hand children are not easy at the best of times. Susan moved and subsequently married Dykie, which lasted for some ten years till he sadly died. One of his last ever-cheery emails, 'don't forget it's hats on boys,' referred to skin cancer, and I am absolutely adamant about this for all sportsmen. For the ladies take note there's no such thing as wrinkle proofing cream, it's either plums or prunes!

So it was NK in NYC in a rented flat for two years until the call of the heather as per the next chapter, which we will leapfrog in time by introducing another mix of summer icing on the cake.

It's called Southampton (aka $marthampton) Long Island, situated in 'the Hamptons'. Around this village, with its boutiques, representation of top-line stores, and Brad, a policeman friend, who is a member of the local Shinnecock Indian tribe, lies an oasis which is covered by the Blue Book. Basically you're in it or you're not... even some of the finest shoreline property anywhere and a stable full of helicopters does not qualify you.

Life revolves around your home (which may be in a surrounding parish), the Meadow Club (tennis on grass courts as good as Wimbledon, supported by a dozen or so pros), the National Golf Club (c.400, er, men only members, and I daren't tell you about the subs), the Southampton Club (men only but ladies can stay as guests) and the Beach Club. Yes gals, here it's hats on for lunch regardless of the usual sun, and even in the 'canteen' when it occasionally pours with rain!

Big Atlantic Ocean on the beach, queuing up for lunch, just like prep school, and each item is charged separately. Try stinging your host for lobster and crab on one plate. The 'old guard' get stuck into corn beef hash, roast turkey and the clam bar, and even hot-dogs and ice cream. Caveat serious people-numbers pollution at the weekends!

Evenings it's all dressy, even informally, and don't the ladies look scrumptious. As one prominent banking heiress told me when I compared this elegance with the dowdy Brit style counterpart, 'Well, you see, Nigel, we work at it'... and she certainly does, with excellent results. For some it's a full-time occupation; you can never be too thin or too rich. Any 'alterations' required, consult Dr John Anton.

Smart summer-evening kit is still de rigueur for the men, and the Southampton evening 'uniform' is white trousers and a blazer. This title now also incorporates what was originally known as a 'boat coat' – blazer really being the stripy, multi-coloured variety worn at cricket matches, and rowing or sailing regattas. Southampton it's ties and no socks, East Hampton the reverse!

WASP spiritual refreshment takes place in the summer at the St Andrew's Dune Church (transformed from a US Coastguard station to a church in 1879 'for those in peril on the sea') situated next door to the Beach Club. White ducks and blazers for the Trustees and leadership from the Revd Peter Larsen, supported on occasions by prominent guest preachers. The C of E needs to import a couple of hundred Peter Larsens, minimum.

Southampton has featured as an annual summer holiday for ages, thanks to my great friends. Other friends come and go... the regulars are just nothing but welcoming. The sad demise of an elderly friend set summer 2006 on a memorable course, occupying his garden cottage for the month of July... his charming Italian widow wants to feel that the place is still alive.

Don't go to the above on spec; the other Hampton venues also feature in *Quest* magazine where you might see your picture… make a start there! [r7]

13 Scotland

'Auld Scotland counts for something still' (Murray)

Manhattan to Moray is certainly quite a contrast, both so diversified in their own respective ways. Sue had visited me in NYC and I had been up to Scotland during the course of trips to the UK over two years... we weren't on a blind date. Her house, of dower house proportions, was situated at the start of the Darnaway Castle drive, which is 1.5 miles long. Everything else belonged to Douglas, Earl of Moray and unofficially we had the run of it. Walks around the woods, through the estate roads, down to the river Findhorn, pheasants, ospreys, capercaillie, pine martens, and two in-house friends, Petal and Rosie – black and cream Labradors! The former could 'shoot'; the latter definitely did not, but both loved walking in the woods and chasing the roe deer.

A syndicate shoot for friends of the estate was right on our doorstep so a natural draw for the most delightful 100ish bird days. The keeping, one head and two beat, for no more than a dozen days' shooting, including house days, was top-of-the-line stuff with the agent able to control the price... so far removed from the greed aspect of 'commercial' days. Jimmy, the head keeper, was a source of amazing knowledge, and combined his position with river watching in the summer on the Darnaway Findhorn beats. We took a day on Thursdays on one of the finest scenic stretches of river anywhere according to experienced guests' comments. We also caught fish... even me who launches a line rather than role-model casting.

One early morning in June, I nearly drowned in a spate. I once was apprehended by a lady house guest when returning for breakfast with a fine ten-pounder and three trout on my tray. 'Did you catch that? – having listened to her and her husband giving us the big fishing spiel the previous evening, and not wanting to bother to come down early the next morning – 'Er, yes,' I replied, 'the fishmonger's not open yet.' My American pal Edward, never having fished for salmon before, had one on and landed inside the first twenty minutes, and on my single-handed 9 ft rod. This is the one that attracts rather sniffy comments from ghillies when arriving as a guest on strange beats.

The whole scenario, supported by the wonderful natural surround-ings, gave everyone great pleasure, and also encouraged other shoot-ing and fishing invitations. I always have a wry smile when 'our fishing trip to Scotland' is discussed around the Sassenach dinner table. 'Oh yaah great fun, no water [alternatives too bright, too much water, muddy water, no fish this year] but maahhvellous scenery.' We could just go down and have a few casts ('nay flee on tha watter, nay fusch'), and for the Scottish scenery bit just look out of the window... it's all still that good.

Another little country pursuit was ferreting with a Harris hawk. These charming birds, originally from the US, get very excited the moment the ferret box comes out and stay very close to the action. They are released into a tree alongside the working ferret and will move down automatically in line with the releases. There's something very appealing when the ferret pops up on a blank run, and one hears the bell on the jesses of the bird moving down a 20-yard interval in anticipation of something better next time. On bolting a rabbit the hawk swoops down and completes the catch. They can just about knock a pheasant over in dense cover, but are relatively slow out in the open as compared with peregrines and other falcons.

I once heard a countryside 'expert' describing how he'd seen a buzzard stooping on and stopping a partridge in full flight. Maybe... but probably not... I ask you! ('A bird in the hand is worth two in the bush.' Amuse yourself by reversing the procedure.)   [b27]

'Well... and how are your reels, Kenyon?' demanded an old friend up from England at the top of his voice, having marched down the centre of Inverness Cathedral in front of a packed congregation waiting for a senior social wedding to start. Answer; just fine, thanks once again to old Mum and those dancing classes. A real domestic must do at the time was to be able to dance the Reel of the 51st, and the others all take a bit of mugging up. You will be familiar with Mairi's Wedding, Hamilton House, Postie's Jig, Machine without Horses, probably? Sassenachs beware, reels are still very much in and ballroom dancing (aka flatties) is not, whether at a local ceilidh or society ball, either private or centred on a society such as Skye, Donside or the Northern Meeting. [b28]

The last was formed as a swells' fun club centred on the counties of Elgin, Inverness, Moray, Nairn and Ross, plus a few likely big landowning qualifiers on the fringe. This group has had only c.2,000 members since inception in 1788, with very few ladies in their own right – my Sue was one. Outdoors, competitions were arranged for Scottish field events and piping competitions, and indoors two balls, summer and winter. Two hundred couples in full flow is very spectac-ular, with men dressed predominately in 'the' kilt (never 'a') and trews, and encouraged to wear 'powder horns and other Highland Dress accoutrements'. The ladies wear sashes and tiaras if possible – 'I always keep Granny's in the bank' – lucky old you. Exposure of cleavage must be limited, unless of outstanding quality, and no slots up the side of the skirts!

Your dances, numbering up to eighteen and all booked on a card, go on till five in the morning – summertime it's broad daylight at 2 a.m. This can become very tedious due to the tradition of always calling for an encore, and even more so if one has a mission for some serious 'chatting up'. Once on a New Year's Eve in a marquee, the portable heating broke down and we were all dancing in overcoats... outside temperature –20 centigrade. Venue: Brodie Castle, home of Ninian, The Brodie of Brodie. [b29]

The Clan Chief of the Mathesons at that time was a certain Major Sir Fergus Matheson of Matheson, Bt. He was ideal in stature and general presence for the role and particularly featured at Clan Gatherings. This involved several days of celebrations and included members from different parts of the world. The day of the Clan Highland Games the members paraded into the grass arena situated in magnificent Highland rural surroundings, the Games were offi-cially opened by the Chief and away we went. An American friend got a great kick out of 'going over to have a word with the heavy men' (various man mountains who toss cabers – a beam the size of a tele-graph pole, and throw stones around – which the average man can hardly pick up) and 'schmoozing with the Mathesons'. He himself was dressed in thick tweed knickerbockers on the hot June day.
('What's worrn under the kilt? There's nothing worrn... it's all in perrfect worrkin' orrder.')

Is Scotland the HQ for golf? Did it start here? Brother Chink is now claiming that they started it! For variety Scotland is unique, and you don't need to be playing on one of the 'greats'. Why does dear old brother Yank insist on jumping off a plane and playing one the same afternoon? Also 'we played ten courses in six days'... oh dear me! [r8]

The smaller ones need preparation and savouring just the same.

Nairn, Dornoch, all very fine, but also consider the Boat of Garten, Fortrose and a fine old 'hairy beast' called Lossiemouth. South of Edinburgh try Gullane ('Gillen') or Muirfield (a member must take you and get him (only!) to treat you to lunch at the weekends), but don't forget Dunbar just down the coast. If you're at Turnberry, just move one down for Stranraer, and so it goes on. It does not always rain... golf in the Highlands is wonderful into October. Gleneagles packages well, but I suppose I'm bound to say that. [r9]

Close exposure to a larger than most private travel company opened up the travel horizons. Sue had started this business from scratch as a general high street travel operation, with strong support from upmarket nobs in Edinburgh and posh Scotland generally. Spouses or partners were sometimes included on 'fam trips'.

Great highlights included a safari in a camp put down for the occasion with *c.*20 huts, 50 supporting staff, and riding on the range. This was used by the Prince of Wales and family the following week, and never put out again. [b30]

A cruise in the Caribbean – never go on one with more than 300 passengers. [r10] Smaller configurations, including European and other rivers, are also fun but must have kindred spirit on board. Try one of those 'gulet' yachts in Turkey, but must be a smart one, and take friends as mates.

I was also able to introduce the 'boss' to more of the US and some good times were had in South Carolina, including the Races at Aiken in March. This is part of a spring series of jumping fixtures, small course/point-to-point style with typical boot (US 'trunk') picnics. The actual racing featured professional jockeys, over plastic fences at hurdling pace, on very hard ground. Aiken also has a real tennis club just off the main street, and the polo boys play winter games en route to the south from the upper East Coast. Palmetto golf course is one of the 'oldies'.

Several runs to South Africa and Zimbabwe gave one a real political/social insight whilst staying with locals. Yes, the day Nelson Mandela dies, hang on to your hats. 'Oooh nah, Cape Town will never be like Joburg'… um, excuse me, it's getting there already.

Business golf was required sometimes, and on a major ABTA conference in Malaga, somebody won the clay pigeon shooting competition. 80 + competitors, a few novices, but conversation such as 'I go to the gun club every Saturday' on the bus, plus obvious special vests, caps and glasses, indicated that there were some pros around.

Political Scotland will come up in our political chapter, but sadly home politics changed tack. Enter the widower, with two attractive teenage daughters. Nice fella, old friend of the family and all that, but we chaps do get a bit cheesed off when outsiders come into the picture. Not that a captain of HMQ's navy, who had also been commanding the Royal Yacht, could ever be described as an outsider. Nevertheless bells sounded, and I was retired up the hill to a bungalow with a wonderful panoramic view and 'could I look after the dogs for a year?'… well, of course I could, what a sport!

Once again the bachelor pad syndrome took over, with the Inverness sleeper train acting as a shuttle to London. Inverness airport, only five country miles away, also provided a hub for overseas flights for incoming guests, sometimes from the US. But the thinness of the Highland social structure encouraged research into other parts of the UK.

14 Middle England, GB and all that

'Where social aspirations rule the head and colour one's judgement' (Anon.)

My re-exposure to day-to-day living in England, after some fifteen years' absence, half US half Scotland, was a surprise to say the least. On the pleasant side, I was living in a Castle (not a stone fairy tale kind, but a fortified house) with Penelope, the kindest of companions, and Bramble, a one-off Springer spaniel.

Every morning at 8.30 prompt he used to leave the extensive garden and head off for the farm next door. A trip round the yard, say hello to the men and his great love, a real farmyard collie called Meg, returning by 9. One night Meg died and Bramble saw her body the next morning. He visited the farm the following day, but never went again, even though Meg had been replaced. His unusually sensitive demeanour was always noticeable whether in the field or by the hearth. He even looked after groups of orphaned lambs.

Outside we had seven peacocks, with numbers expanding every summer. A variety of horses, including racing mares and respective foals, were based around a separate castellated yard. The scene extended to a Park, where one could badger watch on a summer's evening around the wildlife dingle. There was also a trout pond, which provided an instant catch... until one wanted a couple for immediate consumption.

The other side of Hereford there was the farm with a boundary of 2,000 yards of the river Wye. The general wildlife improvements included a tiny pheasant shoot which gave us all much pleasure. No greedy bags or swigging champagne at 11 o'clock, just fun and sense of involvement. The local fox hounds held a meet there, the mink hounds swept down the river and stopped at our fishing hut for midday break. Hedges improved, ponds were cleared which attracted wildfowl galore and, er, somebody actually caught a salmon after a lapse of several years on that part of the river.

On the social front one quickly became aware how the British way of life had been manipulated. This had led to a wider divide in the class system, particularly in more rural areas. Certain sections of the community were fighting a rearguard action, often wafflers wailing into their whisky and some playing the High Sheriff card. This social pass round has also extended to women... one by design.

A friend in Lancashire was asked if he would like to consider the position. 'Oh no thank you very much, but why don't you ask my wife, she's good at that sort of thing'... and she was.

I heard another on her mobile phone, in a crowded railway carriage and in a loud voice, talking for ages to the housekeeper about a dog which had run away and something else about 'I'll call the keeper', which she then did. This was real H. M. Bateman stuff, and a flip remark from me was chewed out with some very unpleasant riposte. Fortunately others – friends, acquaintances and noticeably younger people – have put it behind them having successfully contributed to the running of things... something to do with that 'gut' maybe.

Looking further down the pyramid it became very obvious that there was (and maybe, still is?) a reluctance to let go and embrace the newer wealth of people, not only with money in their pockets, but also proven thrust and ability. This platform had been set up under the governance of Maggie Thatcher, herself from a similar mould, and not called The Iron Lady for nothing. The protective barrier was obvious in political and charitable groups... also on county or national countryside society committees.

I tried to liven this up and stood for the County Council as a Conservative candidate. I went for an interview with the Branch Committee composed of the 'old guard' and, although they said that I would do, they were still going to encourage votes for their old friend who had been in the seat for some thirty years. He flew under the flag of 'Independent', albeit a paid-up Conservative. We lost a sure-fire Conservative seat by 160 votes, and the county continued on its merry old way.

And who were/are the characters on this national stage? In many cases people who had been 'left behind'. They had retired in the 1980s/90s from professional offices as partners, senior management in industry or army and diplomatic positions. What seemed like a comfortable base had been eroded through inflation, mismanagement of pension funds, Lloyd's insurance losses and plain and simply beginning to live longer than expected.

Also, more recently, it became very apparent, this time in the East Midlands, that many of the so-called travelled – 'we've just come back from a cruise', how fascinating – had really only lived in a 25 mile radius, which included home, work, and even boarding school. Listening to conversations about brilliant children, pills and people is a very boring occupation.

Everybody likes to be asked to join in, not just watch, particularly when they have something to offer. Living in a certain place for centuries does not qualify anyone to ring-fence the action to the extent of excluding newcomers, or local people with talent!

15 Party Politics

www.patrioticpoll.co.uk

From a background of mills, trading throughout the Empire, Battles for Britain, Bulldogs and Union Jacks, one was always aware that somebody was in control… or at least trying to be. The King and Queen featured, the National Anthem was played in the cinema and in the theatre, we all stood up. Why? They weren't there… oh well, we were surrounded by conservatism and day-to-day governance reflected on MPs, particularly in such an obvious scenario as Cheshire. Socially acceptable gents, with stacks of character and cash, bags of leadership qualities and gut, were shoo-ins at selection time. They lived in their constituency locality, enjoyed pottering up to London and were able to float along on an economy that was booming on the back of wartime recovery. My awakening to this element of political shamateurism came at the time of the Suez Crisis in 1956.

Great excitement… the Member was coming to a Conservative garden-party thing anyway, but at the same time he would get us in line with the latest news. My mother exhorted worthy bodies to bake cakes, lay out tables for sales of work and raffle prizes (what's new?) and at the appropriate time a black car swept up the drive. The Member, in a thick striped suit for a hot summer's day, appeared on the terrace through double doors to applause, which he acknowledged with victory parade style waving. 'Well, as you all know, we've had a momentous week, and decided, after much deliberation, to invade. [more applause] Now I fully agree with this and on Thursday I got up in the house and told Parliament, "up and at 'em, hit 'em for six!" ' The final delivery was on a Nürnberg decibel scale… even the spaniels looked embarrassed!

With the Israelis going in first as a stalking horse, the British 'invasion' of Suez was a serious debacle, decided unilaterally by a Prime Minister, Anthony Eden, almost at the level of a personal decision. The ground troops were badly equipped (this all sounds a bit à la 2000 and something) and, from a first-hand report, the landing ducks were inadequately armoured on the front end. This meant that they were even vulnerable to small arms fire from either side of the streets. My informant, who was one of the leaders, ended their first run with his sergeant dead in his lap, steering across the driver whose head had come off and the rest of the men being minced up in the back. Of his total load only he and a few others miraculously survived.

My next political encounter was an upgrade in the form of the Prime Minister, Harold 'you've never had it so good' Macmillan, visiting the Mill in 1959. Family all on parade for tea in the canteen, and first in Lady Dorothy… all tweedy and mumsie, flops down in a chair having been on various visits in Bury… Women's Guilds and the like. 'Whew, what an afternoon… yes, I'd love a cup of tea… thank you so much… where's Mac?' On next and (with maximum toffee up your nose) 'Wahl… are you going to cahm into the fahm, boy?' Mumbled 'Well I hope to, sir'… and that was it. Later, after he had retired and passed on the mantle to his totally unsuitable grouse-shooting friend, certain little family, er, indiscretions were revealed. He also declared, whilst sitting in his garden during the course of a personal TV documentary, that if the going looked tough (had he ever looked the word up – the family still features on a 'Rich List') he liked to read some poetry, preferably Shelley. I suppose that in those days travelling only with a secretary, a detective and often by train compared favourably with today's excesses... at least there weren't private jets to fill with great delusions of grandeur!

So the 60s and 70s rolled through on a radical political readjustment see-saw. Socialists upgrading from cloth caps and pints to suits and expense accounts, Conservatives redirecting to grammar school boys and even a lady who started over the chemist's shop. Good for her, the best PM of the second half of the twentieth century. She latterly got a bit carried away, and openly competed with HMQ, and maybe even Churchill when she declared 'A great and glorious victory.'

This referred to the Falkland Islands campaign, when an 'aircraft carrier' was cobbled up out of a cruise ship, and the final assault on Port Stanley was saved by unexpected cloud cover which fortunately appeared halfway through. The weather forecasting was wrong, and the whole evening nearly deteriorated into a total wipe-out. The Argies' antique battle-cruiser, the *Belgrano*, was unnecessarily sunk by British submarines using new style torpedoes with a wire trace ensuring 100% accuracy. Were they also meant to have sunk the two escorting destroyers? Who said that the submarine crash as depicted in *The Hunt for Red October* never happened?... but that's another story!

Ronald 'Hopalong' Reagan and Bill 'Bubba' Clinton provided interesting political-watching during my sojourn in the US. George Bush Snr – Dubyas' pa – came between. I am predicting a Rudy Giuliani versus Hilary Clinton contest in 2008, with Giuliani coming out as the winner… you heard it here!

But it was only on returning to Scotland in 1994 that full recognition of what was happening to GB became apparent. One word: Regionalisation. Was this the test bed for things to come?

Scotland was heading for a quasi independence, politically on a sentiment basis with the SNP (Scottish Nationalist Party), and economically through commercial control being asserted by Scottish Enterprise (based in Glasgow) and its junior brother Highlands & Islands Enterprise (based in Inverness). All industrial aid and development cash from London is channelled through these outlets.

Full independence, albeit still covertly financed from London, was granted by the Labour Government in 1997, with all the trappings of a full-scale Parliament, including an absurd building that cost ten times the budget.

The conduit for this industrial bribery is via LECs (Local Enterprise Companies). These eight fully staffed organisations will support proposals, both public and private, but only on their terms. Their investments (do we mean a herd of white elephants? Latest national UK version: white jumbos, this time jet airliners) have included such ventures as the Great Glen Cattle Ranch, a Funicular Railway running out of Aviemore, disastrous investments in traditional Scottish products such as woollen textiles, business parks with nothing in them except fancy landscaping and an enterprise office, a huge success in a medical company in Inverness (where the seed money was on par with a gift and which has been self-financing ever since) and not to mention the current deficit in the Enterprise accounts running into £millions. Perhaps this is supporting inflation-proof pensions for retired executives and the favourable terms enabling tenants, sometimes just inhabitants, to buy their property from a larger landowner… a forerunner of land socialisation throughout GB?

Personal political curiosity extended to more practical involvement when I managed a friend's campaign standing for the Referendum Party, a protest faction bankrolled by prominent financier Jimmy Goldsmith. Apart from the fun aspect of campaigning in northern SNP-controlled Scotland – bullhorn blaring down the streets, sometimes with riposte such as 'Thank you sir, V for Victory I presume.' 'Quite right, madam, first not second.' – information from all sides gave one a serious wake-up call to an obvious phenomenon – The European Union. From then on, with further canvassing in 2001 when I personally stood for the UKIP (United Kingdom Independence Party) with my Referendum friend, Paddy, acting as my manager, this EU question has moved from a sinister hidden paragraph to title of the book. What's it all about?

The following is mainly taken from *The Patriotic Poll* which I published, and have updated on the internet since 2003. This has attracted a daily intelligence input from a wide-ranging series of official correspondents and private agents. By 10 a.m. one has to pinch oneself hard – welcome to alarming reality on an ever steeper curve!

☞

Throughout the centuries, whether by conquest or diplomatic manoeuvre, there have been various attempts to amalgamate the countries of Europe into a single world power. The twentieth century was no exception with two significant thrusts, instigated by Germany, namely the two World Wars. The re-emergence of Germany as a republic in 1950, under the leadership of Chancellor Konrad Adenauer – a rabid Europhile – set the current initiative on course to create a unified EU (fully integrated membership of GB is a must have) within a timeframe of some fifty years.

In 1954 the Bilderberg Group was formed by Prince Bernhard of the Netherlands and Joseph Retinger to formalise a senior general background for the creation of the EU. This secretive group meets annually, comprising international businessmen, corporatist and socialist politicians, strategic journalists and a few misguided continental royals. Both Heath and Blair attended prior to becoming heads of their respective parties, Romano Prodi in 1980 (he has just surfaced again as Italian PM – watch out!), to name but a few.

The swinging 1960s saw a radical change in British behavioural patterns and various groups hijacked the trends for redirecting the political agenda. By the early 1970s the seeds towards a consolidated 'European Superstate' had been sown. GB entry into the 'Community' was contrived by Edward Heath on the basis that we were joining a 'free trade' area known as EFTA (aka 'sold down the river').

Since that time, with the goalposts gradually changing under the cover of a series of 'Treaties' – Rome, European, Amsterdam, Maastricht and Nice – literally thousands of regulations have been foisted onto the British people without any consultation, other than hasty endorsement by parties with hidden personal, politically-motivated agendas. Under the guidance of such self-promoters, the EU has become a balkanised, fraudulent organisation which has not even had its books signed off over the past eleven years.

Gone!

Our fishing grounds. Given away by Heath – Treaty of Rome – as a bargaining chip in deference to the Spanish, British trawlers have been gradually whittled away. Disregarding recommendations of serious scientific and environmental groups, EU commercial fishing policies are dictated from Brussels. These are supported on a day-to-day basis by the 'fishing capital' of Europe – yes, Vigo in Spain!

Our farming policy. Simply dumbing-down the finest farming systems in the world to accommodate smallholdings and medieval farming practices, thereby creating a marketplace of fraudulent subsidies. 80% of CAP (Common Agricultural Policy) subsidies go to 20% of the producers. Work that one out on a theoretical pot of £100 and 100 farmers! Tobacco growing is subsidised by the EU coffers to the tune of one billion euros p.a. in Greece, the Balkans et al.... and we are stopping smoking in public places, thank goodness. The US have been very stoical about this one. In NYC smoking is banned in all public places, including the smartest social clubs down to the lowest of dives. We are also trying to improve the NHS (health 'rationing', i.e. trying to provide too much, for too many, with too little. Think which word you can control) and continuing with the ever present battle against cancer.

The power of our courts. Now deferring to 'EU Rules', the Napoleonic system of corpus juris. Take two family examples. French law does not necessarily allow you to choose the beneficiaries of your will. The Napoleonic code gives priority to children of the deceased, including children of former marriages. Assets in the UK can be included in judgements related to assets in other parts of the EU.

Going!
Control of armed forces. The 'Rapid Reaction Force', being sold under the spin of terrorist control, all points to a military force under total control from Brussels. The British army regiments are being amalgamated, now down to 101,000 strong... the RAF (48,000) is being forced into buying planes which are over-priced and out of date. Also refurbishing old helicopters to the tune of £10 million apiece, and then they can carry five men! No money for new ones until, er, 2015... and as for the navy, have we got one? (Well, sort of, with only 35,000 personnel.)

System of policing. Europol already established in the Hague. Proposed amalgamation of UK police forces into twelve regions is now under way. (Hey, twelve regions... sounds like a brick in the 'Regionalisation' programme.)

Sovereignty. The Fabian Society, a left-wing pressure group, is promoting proposals to retire HMQ as head of the Church of England. This would be the first step in demoting the British royal family to the has-beens level of their European counterparts. How does this all sit with Blair, who may easily sign on as a full time Roman Catholic when he retires as PM... or with one of his lady ministers who is a member of Opus Dei... or his side-lined mentor who, between breakdowns and other rushes of blood to the head, declared that 'We don't do God.' I can only think that the Deity's response must be 'No, and I don't exactly do you!' Deo dante dedi – Charterhouse motto.

Going!
Our freedom of speech. 'Thou shalt not criticise the EU or anybody therein.' Originating from the Bilderberg Group 2005 agenda (they're still around!) and channelled through the EU there is a proposal for all NGOs (Non-Government Organisations) to register with the Government. Yes... you've got it... this includes your church, gardening club, sports association, political group, social or environ-mental action group, or any non-profit organisation.

Our banking structure. The European Central Bank in Frankfurt will take over all British monetary assets and redistribute. This would also mean setting common interest rates, hence affecting mortgages and pensions. France has an annual wealth tax, currently on a sliding scale .5% to 1.8%. If certain socialists were elected this could rise to 10%. The entire EU inheritance subject is currently under review in Brussels.

Our UK borders. Already crumbling, making England now the second most densely populated country in the world. GB population is expanding at a net rate of 5,000 per week... the idea that 'we need them' – except for a few real specialists – is a myth.

Regionalisation. The EU plans to divide the UK into twelve regions.

This is now under way, regardless of one region, the North-East, having already voted against the principle. Each area is set to host a regional governing body, thereby eliminating county and even parish councils. Ultimately these Regional Chambers will answer directly to Brussels, thereby also eliminating central government in London as we know it. (First thought out in 1933, their proposed boundary demarcations are frighteningly similar.)

The European Broadcasting Union is already in place in Brussels as of two years ago... but of course you knew that already.

Overseeing all this on our behalf are 78 MEPs who go over to Brussels or Strasbourg weekly, sometimes sit in general assembly and press red or green buttons according to their view on legislation which has already been decided anyway... and cost £1.5 million p.p. p.a. to maintain. One, a Conservative who actually favours the EU, has written a book entitled *The Gravy Train* (aka Snouts in the Trough).

All this, and plenty more, can be put in place for good by agreeing to the proposed European Constitution, and this also includes automatic adoption of the euro. There are two signatures of intention on our behalf, by Blair and the now demoted Foreign Secretary Jack Straw. Labour have a core of *c.*40 who are against the idea in its present form. Lib Dems like it, Conservatives hard to read, with an old guard all for it – trying to fulfil lifetime ambition maybe. This decision is achieved either by an enforced 'Parliamentary Vote' (7 so far) or a Referendum (only on offer for 10 of the 25 members – 2 yes and 2 no to date). GB has been promised one. Over 80% of Mr & Mrs Joe Public don't want it in its present format. Collaboration over trade, cultural exchange and common environmental issues is obvious. The last has been a disaster so far with the carbon credits scheme in complete disarray, thereby halving the issue price of coupons from 30 to 16 euros.

And who's waiting to join? Romania and Bulgaria soon... who will be contributing some extra 300,000 migrants to the UK... Turkey and ssshhhh, what about those North African coastline countries? Perhaps that's what Blair meant after he had visited Col. Gaddafi (who showed up in Brussels two weeks later): 'when we welcome Croatia and Africa'.

The problem with real Africa is Africa. Don't send them money, send them goods on a properly planned and sourced business footing. Cash in the hands of power-crazed dictators can only disappear into Swiss bank accounts, finance wives or buy expensive suits... good stuff, but not when it doesn't belong to you.

My first exposure to an African 'potentate' was in Sweden. President Tubman of Liberia was also staying in the Grand Hotel in Stockholm. He arrived in a scruffy tailcoat, accompanied by several women and lackeys all in African costume. Their luggage was very varied including cardboard boxes tied up with binder twine. One was designated, in very scrawly writing, 'President Tubman's hats'. The concierge, also in tailcoats, looked very sniffily at this motley entourage. Through encouragement of inward investment Tubman was on a roll, and by declaring the $US legal tender in Liberia just made life even easier. He died in the London Clinic in 1971, under serious clouds of corruption and brutality, but fortunately no cannibalism featured as with a neighbouring black, self-proclaimed 'King' later on.

What about these celebs jumping on the poverty platforms, particularly on the African continent where starvation and other heart-rending scenes are so obvious? Surely it would be interesting to hear how much they are actually pulling out of their own pockets. Selling more CDs or books for self is one thing, big £/$ donations for start-up and working capital, coupled with obvious hands-on commitment, are another!

And who's been running all this on our behalf for nearly ten years? A captain who has been continuously polishing his propensity for spin* (perhaps good 'actor' might be more appropriate: 'everything he says is wrong and yet he seems to really believe in it'), stayed for free with rich pals, including ex-Italian President Berlusconi, accepted gifts after being valued by the Cabinet Office if over £140 in value... a question of being on good terms with Gus. He's called the Cabinet Secretary, and leads the way talking about 'constitutional and complex issues'.

This charade is backed up by a second minister who is described in the national dailies as 'Two Shags'. Then there was a Home Secretary who had to resign on embarrassing personal matters involving ladies and babies. His replacement was fired soon after for total incompetence, like overseeing the release and disappearance of over 1,000 illegal immigrant criminals, with 179 going on to seriously re-offend, including the sexual assault of minors. (Such pre-meditated actions of assault and murder against all men, women and children are calling for reintroduction of the death penalty loud and clear. In GB in 1820 one could be hanged for shoplifting!)

One lady minister does not know anything about her own personal family finances, like shovelling around hundreds of thousands of £GB on joint signatures with her husband. Another, who helped ruin British farming at the behest of the EU, has now become Foreign Secretary, at least when you see her. When recently visiting Iraq and discussing the question of possible civil war: 'I don't think it's for me to make such an assessment' – oh, I see.

'We'll put it all right'... 'Just a minute, you've been in power nigh on ten years, why let it all get like that in the first place?' Oh, but don't worry, our man in Brussels – aka the EU Trade Commissioner – has four male acolytes... en groupe known as Mandy and his four wives.

Add to this sad scene, lots of cronies who can arrange titles, passports and commercial favours for cash. How's this done? – simple, ask the likely candidates to play tennis and bring their cheque books. Further reinforcement with more Scotties – such as a party chairman 'shit yer face the noo, pah!' and the present Leader of the House (aka Gorbals Mick) 'orrderr orrderr' – is all very encouraging. The ladies have honed up their accents and joined the men in trying to improve the sartorial stakes… opponents are adopting open neck shirts and surrounding themselves with gold-plated tree huggers.

Proper shaving would help across the board, and hopefully in future all politicians can learn to 'keep their peckers in their pants'. This trait must have been inherited from the Lib Dems' own Paddy 'Pantsdown' Ashdown, and the Cons' Cecil Parkinson and John 'I like hot curry' Major.

By the way, windfarming as a sensible business proposition just does not work… full stop. The US spotted that in the 1980s. I watched senior venture capitalists come to that conclusion, and sad rusting monuments, which might be used for a surreal remake of *Don Quixote*, are out there in the western deserts to those who thought otherwise. On the home front, I feel really sorry for sonny boy recently moaning into his mouse mat as to how the family estate is not going to receive a fee of £150k p.a. for doing us the honour of hosting one of these disasters – at least their local planning department seems to have got the right message. I have heard on very good authority that nuclear power does work, now supported by 2006 technology which is completely different from the first efforts starting back in the 1950s… ask brother Frog.

* The current Iraq war was right in principle. It's called getting the lid off the pan and seeing what bubbles out.

At the time of the first Iraq invasion in 1991 everything came to a halt after a few days, even though the baddies were all bottled up in Baghdad. 'Why don't we just go in and finish it and them off?' me to senior American in NYC – whose brother was even more senior. 'Well, Nigel, the US is not particularly concerned with Iraq, the big danger comes from Iran caving in on top of the whole affair. You see, they have a far larger population, as much oil as anybody, but most importantly either have or at least have access to nuclear capability.' Er, yes, quite so and that was fifteen years ago, maybe WMDs sound a bit tamer.

If only the US could get the post-invasion procedure correct. When initially I saw an old General, brought out of retirement especially for the occasion and staggering off the plane with his 'khakis' at half mast, my heart and gut sank.

The 2006 Israeli versus Palestinian sideshow is very déjà vu – see [b31] chapter 12. The early 1980s references in the middle of this extensive tome read like a carbon copy of today's news. On the Israeli side Shimon Peres is still alive, and obviously pushing from the back. Old men trying to fulfil lifetime ambitions are very dangerous beasts!

16 The Back Nine

'They have their exits' (Shakespeare)

Whether we like it or not 65 is the turning point. You've hit the pension, the bus pass and are looking down the tunnel, hopefully with the heavenly light at the end and not just a black hole. The good book tells us that man's life gets to threescore years and ten, and even my standard of maths tells me that this equals seventy. But lifespan would seem to have extended to 80ish, with women still significantly outlasting the men, and quite honestly that's about enough.

(The opposite to this and conditions below were my own parents. Mum died aged 64, of respiratory cancer, whilst Dad merely ran out of steam over a few months to miss 90 by a week. He certainly never flew on one wing as far as the Martini stakes went, but never to excess.)

Think about it. 'Daddy's doing awfully well' – is he? Golf in a buggy, rolling around on a bad hip, driving determinedly with glasses that should have been checked years ago… he probably shouldn't be driving at all. The stick – 'got to carry this ruddy thing' – is laughed off ad nauseam, continually getting left behind, and used for prodding ladies under the dinner table. This is particularly confusing for the recipient when the possibility of a more thrilling approach is anticipated from another quarter. So, the two bywords are old… can't help that, and ill.

Fortunately I have got over the latter hurdle so far. Last ill with a mild dose of mumps at 14 and a recently conquered 'stones' situation still has CNK very much up and running twenty-four hours of the day. (Dum spiro spero – prep school.)

I am told that even in the sixties range this is not always the case, and attributable either to pure anno domini or brewer's droop. This malaise, like alcoholism, is always ardently defended by the wife; if it involves a mistress, the subject gets his marching orders, and pronto. I also have a private medical theory that long affairs with Johnny Barleycorn can lead to a permanent relationship with Al Zeimer… 'oh, nonsense, it's hereditary'… maybe. Regular boozing with the boys is dangerous, and watch out for that white wine box in the fridge, ladies!

Consider how many male and female pals have been affected, often to total demise too early on in the piece. I once helped a friend – we were in our thirties – with this problem, starting with a tortuous summer of sitting with him in the evenings in his very substantial home. His wife and children had pushed off, he had been suspended from the office and just about everything else, and was beginning to break through the two bottles of spirits a day barrier. Luckily this sorry mess came to a head with him breaking down in early September.

His sister-in-law, who had always been in the wings, came back on stage and we were able to persuade him to get help. This involved a serious three months dry-out period in a proper clinic, and except for this intervention our friend would not have made Christmas. He's still alive today!

So, stick to the basics with plenty of exercise; even a good walk does the trick and is miles better than 'jogging'. Try not to run on hard surfaces, yes, it ruins the knees… what a surprise. A few toddies are just fine, and always sleep with the window open, 'unless a better offer comes along, luv', as opined recently by a fine middle-aged body of a nurse, accompanied by your actual Lancastrian nudge and a wink. 'Where's your last report, Mr Kenyon?' 'Oh, er, there isn't one.' It seems as though it's always worthwhile keeping this particular passport current. They seem very keen to do it, to cover their tail as it were, and it's free in the UK. Fortunately on this inaugural occasion no nasties showed up.

As the population gets older, more and more singletons are appearing, with women outnumbering the men. Apart from the true spinster and divorcee, widows begin to feature in our older bachelor/ widowers' market. A word of caution, gentlemen: they are all different breeds of cat.

By this time the spinster will always be the spinster. This is the woman who is not a closet lesbian, but a serious performer at whatever, who finds having men around cumbersome bores, and just could be right! They are highly intelligent at any level and invariably very kind.

The divorcee often has been put on one side in favour of the younger woman. The latter might be a girlie in the office – probably your secretary, or indeed the adventuress with her eye on the till. They must not forget that some ten years later they are probably going to have to cope with the heart attack, transplant or varying degrees of the big C. The ruction was never her fault… in many cases true… but she now has to justify her position, which can lead to gallivanting around with no sense of permanency or commitment.

The widow either just can't bear to be on her own, or finds that being on her own is easier. A third person called 'self' can also creep into this relationship, and that ain't you. She may be well off or have been left startlingly poor, leading to running a b&b or house sitting. A younger model, say third edition, who has had what she thought was a clandestine fling with the yacht's captain, might have been on the receiving end of 'my very best wishes'. This one is girlfriend material only!

Either way a widow is the most understanding of the genre. Smile benignly at constant references to 'Fred' who may have been deceased for ages – too long also is not a good sign – and steady does it on the boboes front. 'I haven't done this for a bit' needs careful approach. Nunc aut nunquam – the Kenyon family motto – is not the one for this occasion!

Beware 'my girlfriends' who will be pouring cold water, or generally poisoning the chalice to portray the enfant terrible – you. This can extend to libellous references. Another danger man is 'just passing'. This is the married man friend who drops by on the way to wherever 'just to see that you are okay'… ha, ha, ha! But when you arrive on the scene, this can change to 'now I've found out something about this chappie.' Plenty of broad shoulders and thick skins needed to repel this onslaught, but remembering Mum's advice maybe: 'don't lose your wool dear, just walk away, they probably don't know any better.'

Also caveat living-in in 'her' house as companion, consort or partner. It's now called Common Law Partner, and any children (at least make sure that they are well established, live out of 'Granny shot', and also no requirements, please, for repairing leaky old rectory roofs or bailing out bolshie brats) will come rushing in imagining you're going to run off with the dosh. This provides fuel for lawyers always looking for new products, and you will receive a thing that looks like a work contract. Who the hell do they think we are, Turkish waiters, ski instructors, tennis coaches or something?!

But we have to keep those games going. Apart from the personal fitness aspect, racquets and clubs are a great catalyst by encouraging doing things together, sometimes in faraway places. Even if 'she' doesn't play, it opens the door for bikinis and bullshit, which they all think they can handle. Unless in very exceptional circumstances, the sell-by date for the former is 50? My runner for a worldwide contest for the over seventies features in the photographs… no misprints, promise, just pure aristocratic class!

Fair to say that after varying degrees of good and bad luck, I have ended up, so far, on the right side. (Fac et spera – Matheson clan) Starting on £4 a week did not equate to a great deal, even in modern terms. Obviously there were the few extras, but they originally went to padding up the difference required to live as a director and active family representative, albeit on office boy's pay.

More adventurous living in the future has sometimes caused hitting the lower end of the scale, to the extent of waiting for that fee, and even a visit on a couple of occasions to 'Uncle'. 'I must remind you that we are a pawnshop and not Sotheby's.' Nothing like rubbing one's nose firmly in the pooh, as if it weren't in there deep enough already. Also, earlier on, a certain Bank Manager, very obviously in the driving seat, was far from encouraging. 'You attract the friendship of millionaires, Mr Kenyon, behave like one, are expected to be so, but unfortunately you are not.'

However, the corner was turned. One could say over the years more like a lap round a very hairy race track, albeit now firmly on the home straight, going looking good. Must have something to do with that 'gut'!

I have achieved no knighthood, OBE (Other Buggers' Efforts), MBE (My Bloody Efforts) or indeed been appointed High Sheriff or DL (Deputy Lieutenant) of a county. The former has more recently been covered by our cousin Timothy Dawson for Berkshire, and the latter by first cousin Suzie Reynolds for Lancashire. Real doers in both cases. Tim and twin brother Nick have achieved so much in enhancing Sunningdale prep school, whilst Suzie helps husband Richard running Leighton Hall, apart from her admirable charity support. Plenty of lead time needed to enter small boys for the first, and you can visit Leighton in the summer... featuring Gillow furniture and their fabulous falconry displays. [r11]

Family continuity is looking thin. My Philip, possibly taking the civil partnership route in due course, is unlikely to be siring any clan leaders, and so it will be up to my nephew Rupert. He has had a familiar run so far, dating his share of society gals and various adventures into the world of showbiz, but fortunately 'Are you in love, nephew?' 'Er no, in lust, Uncle' has taken a turn for the better. His current squeeze has been on the scene for a while, hopefully to graduate soon to a permanent fixture. I am beginning to hold my breath, I once dated her mother!

So how does it all end up? Not yet I hope, and maybe I can get some of those boxes filled. If all else fails, I could ultimately return to Hall House, Fenwick, Ayrshire, now an old folk's home, and depart from the same room where it all began... I don't think so!

Appendices

Eating & Drinking

EATING

A few quickie favourites, culled over some forty years.

Probably just a reminder for many, and maybe you thought of it first. Very likely not, and the same goes for you chefs. Reference to early recipe books of quality – such as Mrs Fairclough, but no direct cribs here – will show that the preparation of food has been adapted and often improved, by using modern ingredients, equipment and time. The last as vital as any, either to save time in the private 'rush', or stuff fat profits into pockets by charging over-inflated prices in so-called restaurants!

Starters

Smoked salmon… as the old Berkeley Buttery? Not quite, that was no egg and a good spoonful of potted shrimps. See what I mean about provenance?

1. Fry 4 brown bread rounds and poach eggs – poaching pans are fine.

2. Mix 1 ripe avocado pear with two good dollops of mayonnaise (homemade for preference, but of course you know how to do that) and a good squirt of lemon juice.

3. Put smoked salmon and egg on fried bread, and cover each serving with sauce.

Consommé CNK – well maybe!

1. Poach eggs (on the sloppy side), put in individual serving bowls to cool.

2. Pour on tinned consommé, having been brewed up with a squeeze of lemon juice and tiny drop of sherry, to jellify around eggs.

3. Top with caviar (fake kind will do) and a sprinkle of parsley.

Soups

Lobster. 1 can (for 2) lobster bisque, Lusty's or Baxters. Add half small lobster body, finely chopped, 1 tablespoon white wine, 1 teaspoon brandy.

Game. 1 can Baxters Royal Game. Add cooked bits of brown game meat, finely chopped. Good tablespoon of sherry. (When Gordon Baxter first brought this out, it was dolled up and served at the smartest of dinner tables. The great Baxter entrepreneurial success story still runs forward, now under the guidance of daughter Audrey, and they're still private!)

Mains

Wiener Schnitzel.

Fresh boned and rolled turkey steaks (thinnish) dipped in egg yolk and breadcrumbs, and fried in hot fat for not too long. Serve with lightly sprinkled topping of coarse mashed hardboiled egg and anchovy. Lemon wedge served on the side for personal taste. This will encourage such female comments as 'wheaah do yah get your veeeal?' (Ready made-up crumbed turkey from the supermarket will NOT do.)

Haddock tartare.
Fresh smoked haddock fillets, check for bones and scissor mash with two knives, leaving flaky. Fork in egg yolk, lemon juice and black pepper. Serve with sauté potatoes and creamed spinach, on the side.

Fast pheasant.
1. Apple puree, on a puddle of bramble jelly, on a warm plate.
2. Flash fry pheasant breasts, 2 per person and two minutes each side. Pile on plate, and serve with spinach salad.

Sweet, dessert or pudding – I prefer pudding!
Ice cream. Takes a bit longer but worth it.
1.5 pints milk… ½ pint cream… 1 tin condensed milk… 4 oz sugar… 6 egg yolks…½ teaspoon vanilla essence.
Milk with eggs into pan… beat eggs into bowl… heat (just under boiling), pour onto eggs. Soon as thickens into custardy stuff add vanilla. Let go cold. Whip cream lightly, blend in condensed milk and fold into custard, lightly stirring for lumps. Freeze. For real piggies, pour on a soupçon of homemade elderflower syrup. Vanilla can be replaced with crushed fruit to taste.

Girlies' flats Chocolate Sauce.
Large Mars bar, thin slices, and into pan. Add half a cup of milk and a good sprinkle of instant coffee granules. Heat slowly, stirring constantly… delicious!

Two fruities.
Quarter fresh, high quality, ripe figs. Cover in bowl with fresh home-squeezed orange juice. Cling wrap bowl and leave in frigo till following evening… et voilà!

Hull strawberries, preferably local. Put in bowl, with mint leaves and good sprinkling of white sugar. Cling wrap and shake bowl around to get sugar well dispersed. Into fridge, morning earliest for evening is enough. Cream and strawberries is a myth, but an accompanying glass of Cointreau (ex deep-freeze like all your freezable liqueurs and vodka) goes down well.

Savouries

Angels on horseback.
Large oysters (clams or mussels will do – sort of), simmered in own liquor till edges curl, but not for too long. Drain and tiewrap each in a piece of bacon. Grill till bacon crisp, serve on white toast.
The big boys' alternative is: dip oysters in egg yolk and breadcrumbs, fry in hot fat, and serve on white fried bread. A good glass of 'Black Velvet' goes well with this variety!

Welsh rarebit.
Grilled cheese on white fried bread, garnished with a good dash of Worcester and a poached egg OR a sardine, with backbone filleted out – as usual, please. Takes no time.

Herring roes on toast.
Simmer roes in butter, with half a teaspoon of Dijon mustard and salt and pepper, until butter absorbed. Serve on white toast and sprinkle with parsley.

In the cooking world, let's forget four letter words and self-publicists, and focus on two real lady cook friends either side of the Atlantic.
Lady Claire Macdonald, wife of clan chief Lord Godfrey Macdonald of Macdonald, and Mrs Victoria Amory, a Spanish aristocrat married to US East Coast establishment figure Minot Amory.
Consult their websites at www.claire-macdonald.com and www.victoriaamory.com respectively. What a breath of fresh air!

DRINKING

There is no excuse for mixing bad drinks, but selecting and serving wine is up to you and the depth of your pocket. Measures and exact quantities can and should be used until one's eye is fully trained, just like food. The following are a further snapshot of fun, satisfying beverages for different times of the day or occasion. Set quantities to suit numbers, here based on 1 bottle for four people where appropriate.

Cold days

1. Mulled red wine. Two bottles of claret to saucepan... plus sliced orange, 12 lumps sugar, 6ish cloves, good pinch grated nutmeg and 6 cinnamon sticks. Bring nearly to boil and stand. Add another pint of boiled water and one good glass of curaçao and one brandy. Chucking ingredients into a bowl, and talking about Gluhwein and some second-rate ski resort, is just 'dead naff'.

2. To one pint of draught Guinness (a tin of 'traditional' will do as second best, but *not* bottled) add a double port, doesn't have to be vintage but even better if so... stir well through. After one of these excellent concoctions you feel well, after two you've probably passed out!

Late nighters

1. Black Velvet. To 1 bottle of champagne add 1 can 'traditional' Guinness, both well chilled. Ideal stirrup-cup, going-home drink (presumably with a chauffeur), or pre beddy byes!

2. King cup. To 1 well-iced bottle of champagne add a quarter bottle of brandy, and nothing else. Only suitable for late at night... definitely pre boboes. (This is not a champagne cocktail gone wrong, believe me.)

Cup coolers

1. Hock cup. Ice into large jug (all mixes for jug, shaker or glass, ice in first – but of course you knew that), 1 liqueur glass curaçao, 2 liqueur glasses brandy, 1 bottle of hock, 1 small bottle of soda water. Lightly stir and add some mint. Substitute champagne for hock and add a glass of apricot brandy, and you have champagne cup.

2. A TT one. For a group where 'I'll just have an orange juice' will feature, why not make it properly. Ice into jug (remember?), 1 pint fresh squeezed orange, juice of 1 lemon, cup of sugar and apricot syrup respectively. Top up with cold water, or half/half water and soda water for a fizzy variety.

Long ones

1. Dark and Stormy. Bottle of ginger beer, good tot of dark rum, squish in a wedge of lime, well iced.

2. Collins... yes, it might be Tom or John, basically gin, but can be whisky, brandy or rum. There is one 'precious' way of making this involving two glasses, let's just stick to one. Shaker, ice in, juice from 1 lemon, sugar syrup (not powdered sugar, please) and gin. Shake, strain to glass, add soda water.

Short ones

1. White Lady. 2 gins to 1 Cointreau, good slug lemon juice, 1 egg white. Definitely shaken not stirred and served in a cocktail glass. The ladies love 'em... and might love you!

2. Ritz Old Fashioned. 3 Bourbons to 1 Grand Marnier, good dash of both lemon and maraschino, shaken and served in chilled glass.

3. Manhattan. 1 rye whisky to 1 Italian vermouth, good dash Angostura. Stir and serve in Old Fashioned glass with a small slice of orange, and squeeze in a maraschino cherry. One of the few cocktails where any form of fruit salad really makes the taste.

(Lemon add-ins should be the squeezed rind and not the whole fruit.)

Mocktails
No disgrace in these, no one knows and they're delicious!
1. Jersey Lily. 1 wine glass sparkling apple juice, 2 good dashes Angostura, small teaspoon castor sugar. Stir or shake on ice, transfer to glass.
2. Temperance. 2 measures lemon juice, 2 good dashes grenadine, 1 egg yolk. Shake through the ice and strain into cocktail glass.
3. Limey. 2 measures lime juice, 1 measure lemon juice, 1 egg white. Shake on ice, strain into cocktail glass.

For further research and extending your repertoire consult:

Henry McNulty, *Vogue Cocktails*, 1982.
Dennis Wheatley, *The Seven Ages of Justerini's*, last reprint 1960.
'Robert', *Cocktails: How to Mix Them*, Herbert Jenkins Ltd., 3 York Street, *c*.1915.
Difficult to locate. The last is one of the founder members of the whole business.

One for the sportsman
A good embrocation for rheumatism, tennis elbow etc. Turpentine, olive oil, and whisky or gin in equal parts. Well mixed, rubbed in after a very hot bath and strapped up with soft padded bandage. Set your mind on it working!

UK Shopping Arcade for the Real Players

Representing proper service, relative good value, and run by proprietors who know what they are doing.

Bookshop
Hatchards
187 Piccadilly, London W1J 9LE. Tel: 0207-439-9921
www.hatchards.co.uk
Established in 1797, Hatchards is one of the oldest and most famous bookshops in Europe and booksellers to the Royal Household. The personal, knowledgeable service in each section is a welcome contrast to the anonymity of larger chain stores.

Chocolates & Truffles
Prestat Ltd.
14 Princes Arcade, Piccadilly, London SW1Y 6DS. Tel: 0207-629-4838
www.prestat.co.uk
www.giftinspiration.com

Founded in 1902, Prestat are England's oldest and most exclusive chocolatier and recognised as purveyors of chocolates to HMQ. Their delicious chocolates and truffles can be ordered online, either to enjoy yourself or as special gifts direct to family or friends. For a real blow-out, a Prestat England Chocolate Hamper should do the trick. They have recently expanded into Singapore, and maybe more to come, to satisfy the Eastern sweet tooth.

Clothes
Cordings
19 Piccadilly, London W1J 0LA. Tel: 0207-734-0830
www.cordings.com
Great country wear and other gents' ready-mades, which can be tweaked if required by your lady in the village who sews, for a real tailored look. Recently resurrected from the fire by rock star Eric Clapton, this 100-plus years' trader only uses British made cloths... and it shows. Also a very good ladies' department.

Cruises
Hebredian International Cruises
Kintail House, Skipton, North Yorks BD23 2DE. Tel: 01756-704-704
www.hebredian,co.uk
Seventeen years ago the *Hebredian Princess* (49 passengers/48 crew) reintroduced the 'Golden Age of Cruising' around the Scottish Isles. This concept has extended to another ship – *Hebredian Spirit* (96/80) – and trips ranging from northern Norway to the Indian Ocean. The 'floating manor house' comfort relating to the number of passengers and the all-inclusive pricing policy must be the preferred option for specialist cruising.

Fishing
Orvis

36a Dover Street, London W1S 4NH. Tel: 0207-499-7496

www.orvis.co.uk or 'Orvis fishing tackle retailers'.

US: 522 Fifth Avenue, New York, NY 10036. Tel: 212-827-0696

Yet another centenarian, with sporting gear and fishing equipment soundly based on the great American outdoors. Their lightweight graphite rods just seem to work, almost on their own! Good practical ladies' wear for that country weekend.

Florist
Edward Goodyear

6 Cathedral Walk, Cardinal Place, London SW1E 5JH.

Tel: 0207-828-1788

www.edwardgoodyear.com

Florists since 1879, by appointment to HMQ and others. Jenifer Emery and her staff really know their stuff, for all aspects of floral presentations.

Garden & Landscape Ornaments
Haddonstone Ltd.

The Forge, East Haddon, Northants NN6 8DB. Tel: 01604-770-771

www.haddonstone.com

US: 201 Heller Place, Bellmawr, NJ 08031. Tel: 856-931-7011

Established in 1971, Haddonstone has expanded to become an international group with offices and manufacturing facilities in both the UK and the US. Their garden ornaments, fountains, statuary and ornamental stonework just ooze quality and style whether in private locations or around public buildings. Orangeries and garden rooms can complete the picture, and look rather different when compared with plastic pimple pretenders stuck on the side of the house. Get your eye in with their magnificent catalogue.

Glassware & China

William Yeoward Crystal

270 King's Road, London SW3 5AW. Tel: 0207-349-7828

www.williamyeowardcrystal.co.uk

US: 41 Madison Avenue – 13th Floor, New York NY 10010.

Tel: 212-532-2358

Who said an artist can't run a business? Yeoward leads from the front on both angles, and has developed his glass designing capabilities into china and other top-of-the-range household products. The custom-made aspect provides for personal heirlooms of the highest quality.

Haircuts

Truefitt & Hill

71 St James's Street, London SW1A 1PH. Tel: 0207-493-2961

www.truefittandhill.co.uk

www.truefittandhill.com – for reference to the USA branches.

Established in 1805 as 'Gentlemen's Hairdressers & Perfumers', Truefitt's can cut one's hair properly according to style required; it's called a 'gentleman's haircut'.

Jewellery & Luxury Goods

Hamilton & Inches

87 George Street, Edinburgh EH2 3EY. Tel: 0131-225-4898

www.hamiltonandinches.com

52 Beauchamp Place, London SW3 1NY. Tel: 0207-589-3215

Scotland's leading jewellery and luxury goods store is independently owned, warrant holder to HMQ and 'one of the most impressive jewellery stores in Europe', which is why we are not featuring Bond Street. To support their fine products, H&I use their own workshops situated above the shop and the talents of designers such as Nathalie Hambro and Annabel Jones. Armchairs and a roaring fire in winter-time complete the picture in their unusual Edwardian showroom.

Outdoor Clothing
John Norris of Perth
21 Victoria Road, Penrith, Cumbria CA11 8HP. Tel: 01768-864-211
www.johnnorris.co.uk
The one-stop shop for top brand waterproofs, fleeces, breeks, you name it. Get their catalogue, give yourself a surprise, and some comfort to your pocket.

Photography
Glyn Satterley
Eriskay, Gosford Road, Longniddry, East Lothian EH 32 0LF.
Tel: 01875-853-103
www.glynsatterley.com
Specialising in landscape and sporting scenes, particularly involving countryside pursuits and their respective estates, his striking black and white images can be ordered from Print Sales on his website. Glyn also works in colour on book and magazine commissions, and for a wide range of clients. These include golf clubs, property agents, hotels and corporate groups. Just look at the website and you'll get the picture!

Playing Cards, Table Games & Accessories
A Pack of Cards
PO Box 297, Tarporley, Cheshire CW6 0WD. Tel: 01829-760-549
www.apackofcards.co.uk
An obvious for bridge buffs through to games for the grandchildren. They will probably pick them up quicker than you, although one is billed for players aged 5-105!

Scottish Meat & Game

Macbeth's

11 Tolbooth St, Forres, Moray IV36 1PH. Tel: 01309-672-254

www.macbeths.com

Mike & Sue Gibson run this meat supply business backed by meat predominately from their own farms, which represent Highland, Beef Shorthorn and Aberdeen Angus cattle. Their supplies of venison, pheasant and guinea fowl are also on the menu in many restaurants, as well as featuring on the grandest of lairds' dinner tables. Argentina and Texas don't even come into the conversation!

Shirts

Frank Rostron Custom Shirts

39 Princess Street, Manchester, Lancs M2 4FN. Tel: 0161-237-9253

www.frankrostron.co.uk

Frank has been making rip-off Jermyn Street look very modest for forty years. Why? Because he has his own sewing facilities, with custom to support sales trips to London, and trunk shows to New York. I was once accosted by an American on the NY subway enquiring about sourcing my shirt supplier – he became a customer!

Shoes

Shipton & Heneage

117 Queenstown Road, Battersea, London SW8 3RH.

Tel: 0870-365-1963

www.shipton.com

Using the best lasts and materials, and sourcing from the finest factories, they supply over 300 styles at great prices. Traditional premium designs compete with fashion loafers, deck and driving shoes – also for ladies. They have recently opened in Paris and Geneva.

Shotguns and Shooting Accessories
John Macnab Ltd.
Macnab House, Haigh Estate, Ross-on-Wye, HR9 7LA.
Tel: 01989-763-859
www.macnab.co.uk
Patrick Keen has his eye on the marketplace, and can source guns if not readily available from the Macnab range or others in stock. Their close involvement with the British Association for Shooting and Conservation focuses on the company's promotion of shooting, very much including young beginners, in the best sportsmanlike traditions. Like our following representation from 'over the border', they have found it unnecessary to diversify into fashion icons.

Dickson & MacNaughton
21 Frederick Street, Edinburgh EH2 2NE. Tel: 0131-225-4218
www.dicksonandmacnaughton.com
Not only suppliers, but able to offer full gunsmithing services on the premises and at their workshop in Dunkeld. The amalgamation of Dickson and MacNaughton in 1999 created the premier shotgun and rifle manufacturer in Scotland, as well as expanding their ability to deal in other peoples' products.

Silverware
Patrick Mavros International
104-106 Fulham Road, London SW3 6HS. Tel: 0207-052-0001
www.patrickmavros.com
Patrick's talents are inspired by the wild animals which live all around the valley surrounding his ranch house home and studios north of Harare in Zimbabwe. He translates this scenario into wonderful silver and other metal copies of animals, either as individual ornaments, or incorporated into practical silverware. Sons Alexander and Forbes look after the GB end, whilst Patrick juggles the sad political atmos-

phere between the two. A ferocious warthog on the end of my favourite cocktail spoon always invokes memories of that valley in happier times.

Smoked Salmon & Other Smoked Foods

Inverawe Smokehouse

Taynuilt, Argyll PA35 1HV. Tel: 01866-822-446

www.inverawesmokery.co.uk

Robert & Rosie Campbell-Preston have built a thriving business – and recently a new smokehouse – over the past thirty years, with head-quarters at their fine home and estate. Their basic products, primarily salmon and trout, are also marketed incorporating imaginative and uncomplicated recipes. The end results leave the Pacific sourced equivalents back in the field.

Stationery, Invitations et al.

CLD Stationery

7 Imperial Studios, Fulham, London SW6 2AG. Tel: 0207-610-9292

www.cldstationery.com

Fancy crested letterheads, all you need for a wedding presentation, and other fine printing and design. For many years Caroline Larken, herself an American, has blended the best of Madison Avenue and Bond Street.

Tennis Books and Memorabilia

Tennis Bookshop

Oaklands Farm Cottage, Oaklands Lane, West Lavington,

West Sussex GU29 0EJ. Tel: 01730-816-116

www.tennisbookshop.com

Alan Chalmers, who has been a Wimbledon Centre Court steward for thirty years, established his racquets sports book emporium in 1988. His stock of *c.*500 racquets sports titles is of high quality, and he stocks no books published after 1935 unless they are in their original dust wrappers. His specialist bibliography now lists over 5,000 items, and this is amended several times per day as new information comes to hand.

Tour Organisers
The Ultimate Travel Company
25-27 Vanston Place, Fulham, London SW6 1AZ. Tel: 0207-386-4646
www.theultimatetravelcompany.co.uk
Tailor-made journeys and escorted tours are big features of this p.l.u. travel organiser. Variety of destinations coupled with diversity of arrangements all blend in with top class guides and internationally acclaimed lecturers. Odds on you will be travelling with kindred spirits!

Travel Agent
Beaver Travel
78 High Street, Forres, Moray IV36 1PQ. Tel: 01309-672-203
www.beavtrav.com
Although operating in northern Scotland with four branches, this private travel agent also services the senior end of the Central Belt, Edinburgh and Glasgow... and books fares nationally throughout GB. It's called service.

Whisky and Wine
Inverarity Vaults Ltd.
Inverarity House, Symington, Scotland ML12 6FT. Tel: 01899-308-000
www.inverarity-vaults.co.uk
Your sporting lodge, home or restaurant should not be without Inverarity Malt or their blended whisky. Patron Hamish Martin also knows his wines which can be delivered as well. No redundant barn operation here, just charming efficiency ably supported by his knowledgeable Scottish staff.

Wine Merchant

Tanners Wine Shippers

26 Wyle Cop, Shrewsbury, Salop SY1 1XD. Tel: 01743-234-455

www.tanners-wines.co.uk

A 160-year-old wine merchant trading at the cutting edge in 2006. The Tanner family, currently Richard and son James, own and run it. Their list and information is seemingly endless about all their fine wines, often privately sourced direct from growers. The four West Midlands shops and warehouse can deliver direct to your UK doorstep in twenty-four hours.

Interesting Books & Other References

b1. Augustus Muir, *The Kenyon Tradition*, W. Heffer & Sons Ltd., 1964.

b2. Gilbert Leighton-Boyce, *A Survey of Early Setters*, private, 1985.
     David Hudson, *Working Pointers & Setters*, Quiller Publishing, 2003.

b3. Jane Nottage, *The Gleneagles Hotel*, Harper Collins, 1999.

b4. R. L. Arrowsmith, *A Charterhouse Miscellany*, Gentry Books, 1982.

b5. R. L. Arrowsmith & B. J. W. Hill, *I Zingari (The Club, Cricket & Characters)*, Quiller Publishing, 2005.

b6. Trudy Baker & Rachel Jones, *Coffee, Tea or Me*, Bantam Books, 1969.

b7. Simon Murray, *Legionnaire*, Sidgwick & Jackson Ltd., 1978.

b8. Adrian Hilton, *The Principality & Power of Europe*, Dorchester House, 2000.

b9. David C. Yallop, *In God's Name*, Bantam Books, 1984.

b10. *A King's Story: HRH Duke of Windsor*, Prion Books, 1951.

b11. Marion Crawford, *Two Little Princesses*, Cassell & Co. Ltd., 1950.
These two will give all the clues about the royal family as it has turned out today.

b12. Julie Summers, *Fearless on Everest*, Weidenfeld & Nicolson, 2000.

b13. Roy McKelvie, *The Queen's Club Story 1886-1996*, Stanley Paul & Co., 1986.

b14. Noel M. Sedgwick, *The Young Shot*, A&C Black, reprint 1961.

b15. Charles C. Norris, *Eastern Upland Shooting*, Countrysport Press, 1946.

b16. Glyn Satterley, *The Highland Game*, Swan Hill Press, 1992.

b17. J. G. Ruffer, *The Big Shots (Edwardian Shooting Parties)*, Debrett's Peerage, 1984.

b18. Ian Copley, *The Music of Charles Wood*, Thames Publishing, 1978.

b19. George H. Guest, *A Guest at Cambridge*, Paraclete Press, 1994.

b20. Sheridan Morley, *A Talent to Amuse*, Pavilion Books, 1969.

b21. Orrin Keepnews & Bill Grauer, *A Pictorial History of Jazz*, Spring Books, 1956.

b22. Whitney Balliet, *American Musicians*, Oxford University Press, 1986.

b23. Nigel Kenyon et al., *The Manchester Tennis & Racquet Club*, private, 1980.

b24. Simon Sebag Montefiore, *Stalin*, Weidenfeld & Nicolson, 2003.

b25. Nick Peto, *Peto's Progress*, Long Barn Books, 2005.

b26. Charlotte Breese, *Hutch*, Bloomsbury Publishing, 1999.

b27. Roger Upton, *Bird in the Hand*, Debrett's Peerage, 1980.

b28. Angus Fairrie, *The Northern Meeting*, Pentland Press, 1988.

b29. Andrew Campbell & Roddy Martine, *The Swinging Sporran*, Penguin Books, 1990.

b30. Jonathan Scott, *Dawn to Dusk*, BBC Books, 1996.

b31. David Yallop, *To the Ends of the Earth*, Jonathan Cape, 1993.

Several of the above are out of print... try www.bookfinder.com or www.abebooks.com.

Quiller Publishing Ltd. have a fun list of sporting books and other jollity, and can be found at www.countrybooksdirect.com.

r1. The National Railway Museum – York. www.nrm.org.uk   The largest in the world!

r2. Cothill House School. Just enter in search.

r3. Charterhouse. www.charterhouse.org.uk

r4. Tennis & Rackets Association. www.tennisandrackets.com

r5. Countryside Societies – which all self-respecting countryside folk should be aware of.
British Association for Shooting and Conservation (BASC). www.basc.org.uk
Council for Preservation of Rural England (CPRE). www.cpre.org.uk
Countryside Alliance (CA). www.countryside-alliance.org
Country Landowners' Association (CLA). www.cla.org.uk
Field magazine. www.thefield.co.cuk
Game Conservancy Trust (GCT). www.gct.org.uk   USA – Email: gbignell@gcusa.org

r6. Zagat Survey. A must-have guide for New York restaurants… other US cities and London. Get one in most good newsagents in NY and elsewhere. www.zagat.com

r7. *Quest* magazine. The 'look at me' East Coast and Palm Beach special. www.quest.com also New York social diary for a daily update! www.nysocialdiary.com

r8. *Scotland the Best!* – the one true guide. By Peter Irvine, Harper Collins from 1993 onwards. Any decent book or tourist shop.

r9. Gleneagles Golf News on the net. All enquiries to mailroom@gleneagles.net.

r10. Silversea. 300 passengers are enough for any cruise ship and Silversea has the answer. www.silversea.com

r11. Leighton Hall. www.leightonhall.co.uk